# TERRORISM: AVOIDANCE AND SURVIVAL

# TERRORISM: AVOIDANCE AND SURVIVAL

 CHESTER L. QUARLES

**BUTTERWORTH–HEINEMANN**
Boston London Oxford Singapore Sydney Toronto Wellington

Recognizing the importance of preserving what has been
written, it is the policy of Butterworth–Heinemann to
have the books it publishes printed on acid-free paper,
and we exert our best efforts to that end.

Library of Congress Cataloging-in-Publication Data

Quarles, Chester L.
    Terrorism : avoidance and survival / Chester L.
Quarles,
        p.   cm.
    Includes bibliographical references and index.
    ISBN 0–7506–9176–X
    1. Terrorism—Prevention.   2. Executives—
Protection.   I. Title.
    HV6431.Q37   1991
362.88—dc20                                    91–16858
                                                   CIP

British Library Cataloging in Publication Data

Quarles, Chester L.
    Terrorism : avoidance and survival.
    I. Title
    363.32

    ISBN 075069176X

Butterworth–Heinemann
80 Montvale Avenue
Stoneham, MA 02180

10  9  8  7  6  5  4  3  2  1

Printed in the United States of America

To a loving wife and supportive family

# ■■ CONTENTS

## APPENDICES—SAMPLE POLICIES

# ■■ INTRODUCTION

The world can seem an awesome and fearsome place. An executive living in an overseas location may suffer tremendous stress because of the lack of personal security and safety. The contemporary business executive must prepare for all reasonable risk. This book is about learning to understand and avoid crime and terrorism in dangerous lands. It is about surviving. This book will discuss pre-incident planning, crisis incidence management, and appropriate post-incident reaction.

In traveling abroad, I learned that international organizations are not prepared to cope with crime and terror. There is a lot of rhetoric about preparation, but there is very little planning, policy-making, or training taking place. Even United States' Ambassadors receive requests from the State Department to learn crime and terrorism avoidance and crisis management skills, but they are not required to attend. Things are not much better in the private sector. This situation is an indictment against our international institutions and is a challenge to the security profession. The security profession must contribute to the solution and not remain a part of the problem. This text is intended to serve as a partial solution through increasing awareness and instilling values appropriate to good policies and procedure.

To deal with terrorism, you need to understand it. Only then can you develop plans, conceptualize policies, and implement crisis management team guidelines. The trouble with many international organizations today is that there are very few plans and even fewer policies to cope with terrorism. Where plans exist, they are often poorly designed and are clearly fallible or deficient. Sometimes the plans are flawed, based on a serious misunderstanding of the terror problem and can cause loss of life. It is so easy to accept a "tough-guy" rhetorical model on terror until your captive is someone that you know and care about. It is hard to keep the no negotiation, no compromise, no concession policy recommended by our government.

This text was researched over a 5-year period. I was role-immersed in terrorism. I read more than 400 books, journals, and professional articles; reviewed thousands of news reports in magazines and newspapers from all over the world; worked on-site in Colombia, Brazil, Ecuador, Mexico, Peru, the Philippines and Pakistan; and interviewed more than 50 terror victims,

43 terrorists or former terrorists, five counter-insurgency military generals, and 16 top police and intelligence officials.

Widely known interviewees included Dr. David Dodge (Lebanon), General and Mrs. James Dozier (Italy), Mr. Richard Grover (Colombia), Mr. Gordon Kennedy (Teheran Embassy), Mrs. Rickey Kirby (Colombia), Mr. and Mrs. Larry and Sis Levin (Lebanon), Mr. Roy Libby (Colombia), Mr. Bruce Olson (Colombia), and Dr. Lloyd Van Vactor (Philippines).

My experiences were shaped primarily by working with a group of men and one woman working with the missionary community. These individuals included Mr. Robert Klamser of Simi Valley, California; Mr. David Farah of Dallas, Texas; Mr. and Mrs. David and Shirley Harpool of Concord, New Hampshire; Dr. Richard Farley of San Diego, California; Mr. Karl Circi of Bodega Bay, California; and Mr. Pat Parks of Petaluma, California. These professionals are team members of great character and determination, as was evidenced as we trained missionaries and relief organization members to avoid difficulty, negotiated for the lives of hostages, and guided organizations through the throes of major crises.

I tried to write this book from a holistic approach. I wanted to deal with terrorism avoidance and prevention programs, as well as the means to combat terrorism. I also wanted to show how plans, policies, and implementation programs can influence terrorist events.

Having personally made mistakes in the field during major crises, I frequently emphasize what *not* to do, as well as what should be done. I have also attempted to approach the problem of dealing with violence from a therapeutic perspective–one that helps the victim, the family, and the organization.

I also deal with hostage negotiation in the international milieu. There are hundreds of articles written about barricade/hostage negotiating in the United States, but very few contributions exist that address a non-domestic terroristic kidnapping. There are few guidelines for negotiation operations in foreign countries and I hope to make a contribution to this literature.

When security programs fail, you should know how to survive. Therefore, I relate the experiences of successful victims. These are the men and women who walked away from captivity with their health and dignity intact.

This book includes historical and analytical studies so that you may understand terrorism. I provide direction for implementing training programs for executives, managers, and sales personnel who live overseas or travel frequently to dangerous locations. This book documents the accomplishments of successful travelers and expatriates and indicates the nature of the mistakes of those who failed.

This book is carefully documented and acknowledges opposing viewpoints. The text shows you how heavily politicalized our thinking is about terrorism and indicates the government's influence on our security reactions to terrorism.

Security specialists from the law enforcement, intelligence, and protective divisions should review their philosophies. What if western governments have published disinformation about certain terror groups? Could western security forces be responding in the wrong way, to the wrong information, at the wrong time? Or using the wrong information at the right time? We can also use the right information at the wrong time.

Buried in the literature and in the debriefings of hundreds of hostages and other terror victims are materials that can benefit potential victims. This book collates the vital information submerged in intelligence files, incident reports, and after-incident audits. This information can help save the lives of future victims.

The book is written for a wide audience—the security executive who wants to prepare his administrators for all reasonable risks, the security trainer responsible for protecting managers, the international entrepreneur who is not yet sufficiently established to have her own security division, and the frequent and occasional traveler. By being aware and prepared for misadventure, you will be in an excellent position to avoid violent incidents entirely.

Even if you should fail to recognize the signals of a criminal or terroristic attack, this book will provide you with some knowledge that could save your life and safeguard corporate property. You can still accomplish the objectives your company has established, even in terror-prone locations.

Security specialists, the executives and managers they serve, and manufacturing facilities located overseas need to be prepared for the difficulties of crime and terror. To accomplish this objective—*organizational readiness*—your corporation needs to analyze, plan, and create an international security policy. As the wrong policy can create havoc during an emergency, several chapters in this book deal with the organization's responsibility to the individual and the work group during times of crisis.

International statistical data was carefully reviewed to create this document. I was often surprised at what I uncovered during my comprehensive analysis. I am convinced that much of what we believe about terrorism is in error. If we react or respond to terror based on our misunderstandings, then we are bound to fail in our plans, policies, and responses, and we increase the chances that our colleagues and friends will die due to our own lack of knowledge or experience.

# PART I:
## ■■ UNDERSTANDING TERRORISM

# 1

## ■■ INTRODUCTION TO TERRORISM

Increasingly, the business community is confronting revolutionaries, guerrillas, terrorists, and criminals. It is now obvious that business is a priority target of these groups. Therefore, it is very important that we learn all we can about terrorism and revolutionary violence to protect our businesses and ourselves. We must learn how to live with it, around it, and through it; we must learn to understand it and predict it.

Business personnel living independently in an overseas environment may be exposed to a unique high-risk environment. Most expatriates and travelers are far removed from the security of the American military; they do not have daily access to the security personnel and equipment of the Embassy.

## ■ THE ESSENTIALS

In the face of escalating tensions created by terrorism and the aftershocks and trauma of violent crime, it becomes essential that international business executives make a constructive and effective effort to gain a better understanding of other cultures and the revolutionary forces within those cultures.

While cultures differ, it is amazing how much people are alike. Citizens of all cultures perceive threats to their security and safety in a negative manner. They long for stability in their homelands. Most people want to be able to provide themselves with necessities, rather than fight.

It is unfortunate that most people rarely react with any understanding in a crisis event. The stress and tension of a terroristic action creates an environment in which all people within a country, race, culture, or religion are negatively stereotyped. Prejudices are often refined in this circumstance. Yet, it is during a crisis that we need more tolerance, understanding, comprehension, and communication. However, it is unlikely that most business personnel will even attempt to attain this understanding.

Prejudice, negative stereotyping, and paranoia are a deadly combination in an international community. These negative qualities exist in all cultures and are almost impossible to overcome, especially in times of crisis. Today, it is imperative that we seek to acquire knowledge and understand terrorism if we are to live or work in a foreign country where it occurs.

# ■ HISTORY

Often, terrorism is treated as a recent concept. The term *terrere* was devised during the French Revolution of the 1790s. But does this mean that terrorism did not exist before that time? Of course not! Historical studies show how little terrorism has changed over the centuries. Perhaps it is only the technology that has improved a terrorist's ability to shock a society. Let us examine terrorism from a historic as well as a security perspective. We will take the data from security systems and programs that were unsuccessful and will examine the security programs that worked and worked well. We will also examine these incidents carefully to determine why some victims survived and others were killed, and will use the security failures to help potential victims survive the tragedy of terroristic and criminal hostage-takings.

# ■ RECENT HISTORY OF TERROR

On October 23, 1983, an unidentified man crashed a suicide bomb truck into a U.S. Marine Corps barracks, destroying the building and killing 241 Marines. The Islamic Jihad claimed credit.

On April 18 of the same year, the U.S. Embassy in Beirut was partially destroyed by a car bomb that killed 86 persons and wounded more than 100 people.

On September 24, 1984, a car bomb exploded at the main entrance of the U.S. Embassy Annex in East Beirut. Fourteen persons were killed. Seventy others, including Ambassador Reginald Bartholomew, were injured. An anonymous telephone caller claimed credit in the name of Islamic Jihad.[1]

On February 7, 1985, the Colombian offices of four U.S. corporations— Xerox, IBM, GTE, and Union Carbide—were damaged by bombs. The Ricardo Franco Front (RFF) and the National Liberation Army (ELN) claimed responsibility.[2]

On June 14, 1985, Shiite terrorists seized TWA Flight 847. Passengers were savagely beaten and an American serviceman was killed. The plane and its passengers were flown back and forth between Algiers and Beirut. The plane and the hostages were held for 17 days as the world watched and prayed.

On October 7, 1985, gunmen seized the Italian cruise ship *Achille Lauro* off Port Said, Egypt. The terrorists took 400 passengers and crew hostage. The hostages represented many different nationalities, but Leon Klinghoffer, an elderly American Jew confined to a wheelchair, was executed and thrown overboard.

On November 6, 1985, guerrillas belonging to the 19th of April Movement (M-19) seized the Colombian Palace of Justice and held it for more than 27 hours. More than 90 people were killed in the incident before government troops assaulted the building. Twelve Supreme Court Justices were killed during this event.

The level of international terrorist activity remained high in 1986, despite a slight decline in the total number of incidents worldwide.[3] However, while there were fewer international attacks, *a greater number of attacks were conducted against U.S. targets.*[4] U.S. casualties were less than in 1985, but the bombing of TWA Flight 840 did not cause it to crash. Two attempted El Al bombings were also unsuccessful.

In 1987, two U.S. missionaries were killed by terrorists in Zimbabwe.[5] Fifteen Americans were kidnapped and released in 1987; five of them were missionaries. There are increasing indications that crimes and terroristic events are being committed against private citizens and businesses instead of soldiers and diplomats. A total of 126 violent incidents took place against Americans in 1987. This figure includes only bombings, attempted bombings, mortar attacks, assassinations, attempted assassinations, assaults, and hostage takings. A total of 4217 terroristic incidents was reported by the International Association of Chiefs of Police (IACP) worldwide for 1987.[6] While American casualties decreased, total deaths were up 106.8% and the total number of victims increased 73.8%.[7]

Total Incidents

| Year | # of Incidents |
|------|----------------|
| 1984 | 2679 |
| 1985 | 2818 |
| 1986 | 3801 |
| 1987 | 4217[8] |
| 1988 | 4343[9] |

Nineteen eighty-eight statistics show that Colombia, Peru, El Salvador, and Chile were the most dangerous countries for Americans, although, most of the events involved property damage rather than loss of life. Analysts predicted that terrorism in 1989 and 1990 would *increase* as terrorists regrouped due to some of the law enforcement and military successes of 1986 and 1987[10] although it was noted in "A Pause in Terror" that this prediction was invalid.[11]

Nineteen eighty-nine statistics indicate that the Latin American region continues to display the most anti-American behavior. Colombia continues to be the most dangerous country for Americans, while Peru, Bolivia, El Salvador, and Chile are high-threat environments for Americans. There were eight incidents in the Dominican Republic, as well. However, in 1989,

Africa had the largest number of lives lost by locals due to revolutionary violence and insurgency.

Scientific analysis of terrorism trends are not reassuring. The data plainly indicate that terrorism is increasing and that multiple deaths are increasing.[12]

While terrorism continues to be a relatively small problem when its victims are compared to the number of victims of war, natural catastrophes, traffic accidents, and crime, there is increasing apprehension about the incredible violence that many terrorist groups inflict.

More Americans were killed by terrorists in 1988 than in any year since 1983. Nineteen eighty-three was exceptionally violent, because multiple fatalities occurred in Beirut, at the Marine barracks and at the Embassy. While the total number of deaths for all nationalities was lower in 1988 than in 1987, there is still considerable reason for concern, due to the 3% increase in terroristic incidents between 1987 and 1988. The Middle East continues to predominate insofar as the total number of terroristic incidents are concerned, but the Latin American countries continue to target more Americans with their violence.

Terrorists were responsible for three spectacular events in 1988—the hijacking of a Kuwaiti airliner in April, the attack on a Greek day-excursion ship off the coast of Greece in July, and, most likely, the bombing of Pan Am Flight 103 over Scotland in December.[13]

An interesting observation of terrorism over the last few years is the shift in targets. Up until 1983, the four primary targets attacked by terrorists included those facilities used by the military, government, diplomatic corps, and business. Today, the fifth category, "Other," runs a higher risk of a terrorist attack as indicated by U.S. State Department data for 1983, 1984, 1985, 1986, 1987, and 1988.[14] "Other" targets include private individuals, missionaries, small business owners, and international marketing personnel. However anti-U.S. attacks continue to target business operations.[15]

## ■ TRAVELERS

Tourists are increasingly being subjected to incredible levels of violence. In fact, the travel industry was severely impacted in 1986; some European areas had a 60% decrease in American tourism. One 1983 study by Rand's research group found that the terroristic activity directed against ordinary citizens increased by 68%.[16] The proportion of violent incidents with multiple fatalities rose dramatically from a 33% increase in 1982 to a 59% increase in 1983.[17]

Travelers are excellent victims from a terrorist perspective. A boatload of tourists from Africa, Asia, the Middle East, Europe, and the United Kingdom assures any terrorist of instant accessibility to the media and of having a worldwide audience. This is what the revolutionary wants. He wants attention to his plight as he fights for cultural and political legitimacy.

Holding a single person or an entire group hostage also has another benefit for the terrorist. He not only gets the media's attention to promote his social, economic, and political platform, but he can also use the hostages for ransom purposes. In the TWA Flight 847 skyjacking, there were reports of passenger robbery. Nearly $250,000 in cash, jewelry, and other valuables were taken from the hostages.

The most highly publicized tourist attack involved TWA Flight 847. During this event, a Navy diver named Robert Dean Stetham, was beaten to death by a Lebanese militant. Several books were written as a result of this experience. Pilot John Testrake wrote a book entitled *Triumph Over Terror on Flight 847*. Co-pilot Christian Zimmerman wrote *Hostage in a Hostage World*. Passenger Kurt Carlson wrote *One American Must Die*. Each of these men learned about terror the hard way, during the events relating to this ordeal. Individually and collectively they share many details important to every traveller. These books are referenced carefully in the skyjacking and captivity survival sections of this book.

## ■ BUSINESSPEOPLE

Increasingly, businesspeople living abroad are also being abducted, victimized, and murdered. Often they are selected because of their perceived financial status. On many occasions they are selected because they are westerners and are surrogate representatives of western life, values, and culture. In some cases, they are kidnapped or targeted simply because they are Americans.

More than half of the 537 Americans kidnapped abroad between the years 1970 and 1978 were businesspeople, not military or government personnel.[18]

In some situations, a business is perceived to be a threat to an indigenous nationalistic group. Poverty, for example, is a powerful stimulant for violent behavior. Therefore, the business organization that is improving the quality of life in an impoverished area may be perceived as a threat by revolutionary groups.

If the needs of the people are satisfied through legitimate means, they will not revolt. Revolutionaries want revolution, so any settling or stabilizing influences in the country will be resisted. Many of these violent groups do not want the economy to improve or want more and better jobs for their people. Many of these terror groups do not even want hunger alleviated. Some of these groups want revolution to such a strong degree that they will kill or capture those seeking to aid the people or the economy in any way.

An attack against a group supplying vital services is called *anti-development terrorism*. Anti-development violence includes all forms of terrorism against those who are helping bring jobs, food, and modern technologies to developing nations. The primary forms of violence used in anti-development terrorism include hostage-taking, bombings, and assassinations.

Claude Fly was one of the most prominent examples of anti-development terrorism. Dr. Fly, a U.S. agronomist was held as a political hostage for 210 days in Uruguay. Dr. Fly, a committed Christian, later wrote *No Hope But God* about his captivity. He was released only after having a heart attack in his cell.

# ■ REFERENCES

1. U.S. Department of State, *Patterns of Global Terrorism 1984* (Washington: Office of the Ambassador-at-Large for Counterterrorism, November 1985), 26.
2. U.S. Department of State, *Terror Attacks on U.S. Businesses Abroad* (Washington: Department of State Publication 9705, Office of the Secretary of State, Ambassador-at-Large for Counterterrorism, March 1986), 11-12.
3. U.S. Department of State, *Patterns of Global Terrorism: 1986* (Washington: Office of the Ambassador-at-Large for Counterterrorism, January 1988), 1.
4. Ibid., 1.
5. U.S. Department of State, *Significant Incidents of Political Violence Against Americans, 1987* (Washington: Department of State Publication 9644, Bureau of Diplomatic Security, April 1988), 3.
6. James Stinson, "Terroristic Tactics: Future Trends" Presented at the International Association of Chiefs of Police Symposium, "Terrorism 2000: Academic, Political and Police Dimensions" (March 31-April 1, 1988).
7. Ibid.
8. Ibid.
9. Stinson's figures multiplied by the 3% factor listed in U.S. Department of State, *Patterns of Global Terrorism: 1988* (Washington: Department of State Publication 9705, Office of the Secretary of State, Ambassador-at-Large for Counterterrorism, March 1989), 9.
10. Mary Jackie Jones, U.S. State Department at Annual Terrorism Conference of the American Society for Industrial Security (March 28, 1989).
11. Chester L. Quarles, "A Pause in Terror," *Security Management* (Arlington, VA: American Society of Industrial Security, January 1991) 35(1), 26-30.
12. Stinson, March 31-April 1, 1988.
13. U.S. Department of State, *Patterns of Global Terrorism: 1988* (Washington: Office of the Ambassador-at-Large for Counterterrorism, March 1989), 1.
14. Ibid., 2.
15. Ibid., 5.
16. Bonnie Cordes, Bruce Hoffman, Brian Jenkins, Konrad Kellen, Sue Moran,

and William Sater, *Trends in International Terrorism, 1982-1983* (Santa Monica, CA: Rand Corporation, August 1984), v.

17. Ibid., 6.
18. Robert K. Spear and D. Michael Moak, *Surviving Hostage Situations* (Leavenworth, KS: Universal Force Dynamics, 1989), 110.

# 2

# ■■ RELIGIOUS ROOTS OF TERRORISM

Surely every theologian cringes when he reads that Christian Protestants and Christian Catholics are killing each other in Ireland. It is depressing to see Christian gunmen engage Muslim extremists in many middle-eastern fights. Jewish soldiers often use violence against enemies within their country, as well.

In other parts of the world, religious fanatics assassinated Gandhi in India (a Sikh) and Sadat in Egypt (a Shia). An attempt was also made on the Pope of the Roman Catholic Church by another fanatic. Some would call the Pope's hitman a religious zealot.

Many observers propose that it is a *Messianic* belief that causes terrorism among and between the Jews, Christians, and Muslims. Basically, this philosophy includes the perception that a Messiah (Christians and Jews) or the Mahdi (Muslims) will transform the earth.

> A messianic belief is one which visualizes a day in which history or life on *this* earth will be transformed totally and irreversibly from a condition of perpetual strife which we have all experienced to one of perfect harmony that many dream about, where there will be no sickness or tears, where we will be totally *liberated* from all rules, a condition of perfect freedom.[1]

Professor David Rappaport of the University of California has noted the recent trend of theological concepts to justify terroristic activity. He calls this phenomenon *Holy Terror*.[2] This concept and term was used to describe a television news series on terrorism. The title was then carried into the popular literature.

Examples of Holy Terror include the revolution in Iran, the collapse of Lebanon, and the use of suicide pacts among Muslims of the Moro groups of the Philippines. The Sultan of Sulu gathered his supporters and claimed a *jihad*, a war for the faith. Muslims in the Philippines began their jihad using the practice of *Juramentado*, fighting in the way of God. Westerners would call the same practice a formalized military suicide.

> After some initiation rites and prayers, the juramentados rushed their enemies with suicidal risks, sacrificing themselves in battle. These men were then memorialized and were believed to be given a special place in heaven.[3]

The juramentado concept was used by the ancient assassins and recently by the Iranian Mullahs on Iran-Iraqi battlefields. The Japanese Army likewise trained its suicide bomber pilots as kamikazes.

The fighting in the Grand Mosque of Mecca in 1979 was based on a millenarian theme as was, conceivably, the Iranian Revolution. Many people in the English-speaking world are being subliminally encouraged that a great religious war is occurring. They believe that religious zeal and the ultimate forms of bigotry are the main sources for hatred, violence, and terror. Even the white supremist groups in the United States claim religious precepts to justify their hatred and their violence as they seek to bring about the millennium.

As we add up Christian-Jewish-Muslim violence and the results of this violence, it may seem apparent that terrorism is a result of religious fervor. Most scholars, however, believe that the concept of a religious war or Holy War is a myth. When carefully examined, terrorists have other motivations and interests toward which they promote violence. These motivations normally include three factors:

1. nationalistic interests
2. ethnic-minority interests
3. economic interests (along revolutionary Marxist Leninist or Maoist tendencies)

Most terrorism is territorial or nationalistic in its intent or focus. *The real issue is land and the power to hold it, use it, and benefit from it.*

## ■ THE GNOSTIC REVOLUTION

Talmudic Scholar Moshe Amon recently developed a theology for terrorism. He described terrorists within a religious perspective in which he has three genres: messianic, gnostic, and apocalyptic.

These religious terror units represent the *attributes* of the world to come. These groups claim to know the nature of the ideal world, even the identity of the Messiah (Mahdi). This knowledge comes from a conviction that they have "seen the light" and are, therefore, the only enlightened people. Terrorists choose to look at the seamy side of society, which they believe reflects the whole of society. They have the inner certainty that the world is hopeless and cannot be mended. They believe the world is suffused with evil; they propose to demolish it and build something new out of the remains.

Their belief that they are the only ones to represent the power of light stems from the conviction that they are the only people who see the real world and are not affected by its depravity. It is their mission, therefore, to liberate the blind people of this world from the rule of the unjust. Through this action, they are rendering justice in an unjust world.

The gnostic believes that if he is armed with the right kind of knowledge, he must destroy the present order to make room for the *final order*. In this respect, terrorists share the destructive attributes of the anarchist and the nihilist who seek to destroy contemporary society. The gnostic believes that he has the right to destroy society, because society, with its crime and corruption, has no right to exist.

All discerning is based on the gnostic's sense of morality. Gnostic righteousness breeds violence by simply reasoning that all people who are not "right" are "wrong." Gnostics believe there are no innocents in the world, thus the "wrong" people have no morally justifiable reason to live. Citizens do not deserve to be reindoctrinated into gnostic theology or even reeducated. They must be *eliminated*. Liberation theology often transcends into these rationales as incredible violence is intensified against innocents.

> Opposing groups are viewed as representatives of the adversary power, that is, the devil. Terrorism thus serves [under this philosophy] both as a means to fight Satan . . . and a way to find fraternity and solidarity.[4]
>
> Gordon Kennedy, a U.S. State Department official, was among the hostages held in Teheran, Iran, for 444 days. He said, "terrorists who base their actions on religion or ideology often argue their case with statements like these:"

> - My beliefs are right.
> - Therefore I can use force or any other means to make you accept my ideas.
> - I will not compromise my ideas to make them more acceptable to you.
> - Those who share my beliefs are my friends.
> - Those who oppose my beliefs are enemies.
> - Those who stand in the way are enemies.
> - To attack those enemies is a good thing.
> - Since I am right and you are wrong, I do not have to consider any of your arguments or beliefs, even if it means we never resolve our differences or end up in a bloody quarrel.[5]

Gnostics often place themselves on the same level as an Avenging Angel of God, as they attempt to break down evil systems. The Antinomian is a believer in the doctrine that faith alone, not obedience to the moral law, is necessary for salvation. The Antinomian Revolution is a liberation from evil systems. The order of things that produced the realities today must be eliminated. Thus we have Democracy versus Marxism, Israelis versus Palestinians, and liberators versus dictators. The ultimate knowledge is the *Epistēmē*. The Epistēmē can be applied for the good of the world when the evil system is destroyed.

## ■ THE NEW-SOCIETY MOVEMENT

There is now a faction within the Roman Catholic Church that has impacted economics, politics, and religion. The philosophy of the group is called *Liberation Theology*. Writer Michael Dobson contends that the theology of liberation essentially grew out of the Roman Catholic Church's involvement with the working class poor in Latin America. He writes,

> For most worker-priests, direct involvement was a profoundly unsettling experience. They soon realized that the church was alienated from the poor and they began to see both religion and social order through a Marxian lens.
>
> Their church appeared as an agent of pacification and cooptation in the absence of any effort to change or draw attention to the real-life situation of the poor and the structural causes responsible for their plight. The clergy became radicalized by their experience and those who wished to bring about changes from within the church had to reassess the priestly vocation, the mission of the church, and the very meaning of faith itself.[6]

Today, there are increasing examples of militancy in many countries. Journalists and other writers have a tremendous influence on the attitude of the people toward helping the poor and the development of food, health, sanitation, land reform, and other social programs for the needy. But instead of passively influencing the development of appropriate social programs, the liberation theologist demands change with a machine gun in his hand and a New Testament in his pocket.

There are many religious organizations that seem to be turning toward Liberation Theology. Many of the old-line, gospel-preaching, Protestant denominations have turned toward this movement. Just as the Catholic Liberationists, Protestant denominations often create "Basic Christian Communities" in Latin America, the Philippines, as well as in other developing nations throughout the world.

## ■ AN ISLAMIC MESSIANIC THEME

Many Muslims share the belief that a leader will come to lead Islam to a new and greater era. The new era will bring the Islamic believer and the religious person back to a worldwide prominence. Shia fundamentalists say that the leader is to be called a *Mahdi*. At the time the Mahdi appears, ancient Shia prophesies record that a world catastrophe will "stimulate those anticipations."[7] It is in this way that millennialistic tendencies influence fundamentalistic Islamic thought.

Ancient Islamic prophesies state that the Mahdi will emerge at the beginning of a new century. In reviewing this concept the reader must understand that the Islamic calendar is different from the Christian calendar used in most parts of the world. It was in this context that some Islamic believers attempted to force a confrontation that they believed would bring about the new millennium.

In the first hour of the first day of the Islamic year 1400, some twelve attackers took control of the Grand Mosque of Mecca. This event occurred in the Christian year 1979. The twelve attackers were from twelve countries *(including the U.S.)*. They named one of their number as the Mahdi. The Mahdi prophesy also made many contributions to the development of the cult of Assassins in Syria and Persia (Iran and Iraq) in the Christian calendar year 1090. It also influenced many themes of the Shia Sect of Islam.

Islam has experienced religious revivals based on the anticipation that a Mahdi will come and that a specter of world catastrophe will stimulate the millennialistic participation as it does with other religions of the world. Christians also have millennialistic expectations and work toward the final order. It is alleged that American Christian messianic groups (who may be interested in creating conditions appropriate for Armageddon) have financed third-temple enterprises in Israel such as the Temple Mount Plot.

The Temple Mount Plot was a conspiracy to destroy a sacred Muslim shrine built on Judaism's holiest site, that of the Second Temple. If The Dome of the Rock site was obliterated, the construction of a Third Temple would be possible—a circumstance that some see as a precondition of the coming of the Messiah. But the destruction of the "Dome of The Rock" Islamic structure would most certainly create havoc between Jews, Christians, and Muslims. Some predict the beginning of World War III or even the beginning of Armageddon due to the destruction of this shrine.

# ■ HISTORICAL EXAMPLES OF RELIGIOUS TERROR

## The Ismaili Assassins

The Ismaili Assassins were a sect of the Shiite tradition and they waged a terror campaign against individual government and Sunni leaders. Their campaign of terror lasted for 185 years and occurred between 1090 and 1275. The Assassins influenced politics and religion for most of the years of the sect's existence. Assassin targets included the Seljuk Empire, which spread from Mesopotamia into Central Asia. They also targeted many of the military leaders of the Crusades. As the region is still inhabited by many Assassin descendants, some observers believe that the group still exists.

The Ismaili Assassins are believed to have been brought to prominence by a young Persian Shiite named Hassan ibn-al Sabbah, an Ismaili missionary to Iran. He joined the group in 1071 and became the first Grand Master of the Assassins. The members of the Assassins were Persians of the Ismaili sect who were all Shia. The Assassins were called *feda'is* or *fedayeen* throughout much of the Middle East and even in certain regions of Europe. The term *fedayeen* continues to be used by certain groups within the Palestine Liberation Organization (PLO) infrastructure as well as by some Marxist/Leninist urban terrorists in Iran.

The Ismaili were a conservative sect of the Shia and the Shia were a conservative division (about 10%) of Islamic thought. The Sunni and the Shias fought at Carbola over who would lead Islam after Muhammad died. Since that time, there has been a major Islamic schism. The heads of the Ismaili sect claimed to be Imams (religious leaders), as descendants of Ismail Ibn Ja'far and, through him, descendants of the Prophet Muhammad by his daughter Fatima and his son-in-law Ali. The Imam is central to the Ismaili system.

The Ismailis offered respect for the Koran, but differed in their interpretation from other Shia. In earlier generations, the Ismailis had a reputation for scholarship and a quest for learning science, geography, and philosophy. As intellectuals, they offered a philosophical explanation of the universe, drawing on the sources of ancient and neoplatonic thought.

The Ismailis were a very secret society with a system of oaths and initiations, and a graded hierarchy of rank and knowledge. Their secrets were well-kept and information about them is fragmentary and confused.

From the end of the 11th Century, the Ismailis fought the Islamic Sunni and the Seljuk military forces, their religious and political opponents. The Assassins were believed to be a multi-classed coalition, including a few members from the families of notables dedicated to a fundamentally millenarian fanaticism.

The "Old Man" wanted the Daylamis people, who lived in the area surrounding his mountain, to believe that Alamut was the door to paradise. He taught that only through the Fortress of Alamut could paradise be entered. Only candidates for the Assassin position were allowed to enter the door of Alamut Castle. These young men from neighboring Daylamis areas were from 12 to 20 years of age. While dining and drinking, Sabbah would drug them. When they awoke, they would be in a beautiful garden and their every need and fantasy were met. It was here that these men were introduced to hashish.

Hashish was the original word form from which these killers got their name. The Assassins began as *Hashishmen*. The term then transcended in the literature to *Ashishmen* and finally ended up as *Assassin*. The term was initiated because hashish was systematically ingested by Sabbah's group.

While these men were in a drug-influenced state, Sabbah persuaded them that he alone held the key to the doors of Paradise. If they gave up their lives for his cause, they were promised a very special and heavenly reward in heaven. These young men, and some women, were indoctrinated carefully, just as the contemporary cults influence their own members. The

Assassins were influenced to accept a very unusual belief system. Many of them gladly gave up their lives while following Sabbah's orders. To commit all of their murders, in Persia and Syria, the Assassins always used a dagger, never poison or other weapons, though there must have been occasions when these means would have been easier and safer.

When an assignment was given to a convert, Sabbah would bless the knives issued for a killing and bless the Assassin. In many ways, this event was like an early funeral service, because the assassin would calmly wait capture and execution rather than flee. They had been issued hashish as a balm for their nerves and to increase their courage.

In some way, Islamic fundamentalists do the same thing today. The Ayatollah Khomeini preached that all of his soldiers would share a special place in the Islamic Paradise (or heaven). Their militancy and violence was spiritualized in the religious sense of the word. The victims of this violence were Sunni rivals who had abandoned the true faith of Islam.

Alamut was taken over, for a time, by the Moguls. In 1275, it was recaptured. The Moguls then destroyed it totally. The remaining Assassins disappeared. Some were absorbed into the local population, some fled to India where they made converts and became known as Khojas—a peaceful community whose members preferred to forget the ways of violence.

The Biqua Valley of Lebanon, today, houses several terrorist groups and their hostages. Perhaps the Biqua Valley has replaced the Valley of Alamut. This branch of terrorism will never cease until the day that Sabbah loses his last disciple.

## The Sicarri and the Zealots

The first messianic violence was caused by a group of Jews during the Sicarri/Zealot Revolution. The Jewish millenarian theme was very violent. These men and women attempted to induce the social coordinates that would necessitate the coming of a Messiah to liberate the Hebrew nation from Rome. The Zealots began a Holy War that induced a massive revolt against Rome. This conflict culminated in a mass suicide at Masada, where nearly 900 men, women, and children chose to die by their own hand rather than suffer at the hands of the Romans.

The Sicarri were the revolutionary arm of conservative Judaism. These men acted in public and during major social events, Roman holidays, and Jewish holy days. Normally, they would attack a prominent Roman, but many moderate Jews were attacked as well. The Sicarri and Zealots led actions that were repressed by Roman authority.

In many ways, the Jewish contributions to Julius Caesar's revolution, as well as those of successive emperors, placed the Jewish community in an enviable position. Jews were exempt from military conscription and from answering judicial summonses on the Sabbath. Jewish communities were given a separate, unique status with the right to settle internal legal controversies.

Rome repressed the local citizenry as it sought to control the Zealots, the Essenes, and the Sicarri. All efforts to find political solutions to Jewish problems were sabotaged by the Sicarri. The purpose of the Sicarri, like many revolutionary groups today, seemed to be oriented toward creating government repression so that the Jews would be forced to rebel. In this, at least, the Sicarri were successful. The Jews revolted under Rome's repressive responses to the acts of the Sicarri, the Zealots and the Essenes. At one point, the Jews successfully besieged a Roman garrison at Jerusalem and massacred all of the soldiers after they had promised them safe passage and the Romans had marched out of their fortifications without weapons or armor.

The Romans counter-attacked the Jews and the Greeks responded by killing many Jews in communities all over the Empire. This began the Diaspora (the Third Dispersal) that scattered the Jews all over the world.

The Sicarri's dream that God would send the Messiah to initiate the millennium was never completed in the ways this group intended. The Jews believed in a Kingdom of God on earth, as do so many contemporary revolutionaries. Many Jews perished because of this belief.

## ■ REFERENCES

1. Paul Wilkinson and Alasdair M. Stewart, *Contemporary Research on Terrorism* (Aberdeen, United Kingdom: The University Press, 1987), 74.
2. David Rappaport. "Fear and Trembling: Terrorism in Three Religious Traditions," *American Political Science Review* 78(3) (September 1984), 658-677.
3. Stephen Frederick Dale, "Religious Suicide in Islamic Asia: Anticolonial Terrorism in India, Indonesia and the Philippines," *The Journal of Conflict Resolution* 32(1) (March 1988) 52.
4. Moshe Amon, "The Unraveling of the Myth of Progress," *The Morality of Terrorism: Religious and Secular Justifications,* edited by David C. Rappaport and Yonah Alexander (New York: Pergamon Press, 1982), 69.
5. Terrell E. Arnold and Moorehead Kennedy, *Think About Terrorism: The New Warfare* (New York: Walker and Company, 1988), 14.
6. Michael Dodson, "Prophetic Politics and Political Theory," *Contemporary Research on Terrorism,* edited by Paul Wilkinson and Alasdair M. Stewart (Aberdeen, United Kingdom: The University Press, 1987), 48.
7. Wilkinson and Stewart, 77.

# 3

## ■■ TERRORISM AND TERRORISTS

One layman definition of terrorism is that it is the systematic use of violence or the threat of violence to achieve political, social, or economic goals. One of the real problems of dealing with terrorism is that it is very difficult to define. The United Nations does not want to describe terrorists as an oppressed people fighting for real freedom from oppression.

Developing nations who use state terror tactics want to be formally identified as the legitimate authority for their country. During the last three decades, more than 103 definitions of terrorism have been published in government publications studying terrorism and revolutionary activity. The definition is primarily influenced by political friendships. If you are my friend your state terror is justified. If you are not my friend your state repression is abhorred.

Is a legitimate government able to define all of its violent challengers as terrorists? Should a mistreated and oppressed population be labeled *terroristic* because they rebel against wrongful taxation and government corruption at high levels?

Generally, terrorism is considered to be any act performed by an individual or by a group that is designed to undermine the legitimate authority of a government or state. While terrorism was rarely encountered a few decades ago, it is now a rather remarkable trend. It is often the first weapon selected against a government by people seeking legitimate freedoms or by subversives seeking to overthrow a government or its economy.

Definition problems have plagued scholars as well as politicians. In the United Nations, one popular axiom is "one man's guerilla is another man's freedom fighter." For the purposes of this book, the terms *guerilla, freedom fighter, criminal,* and *terrorist* are not at all synonymous. While any violent crime instills terror, there is a considerable difference between a crime such as rape, which is terrifying, and the indiscriminate application of terror as a tactic and as a weapon. There is a considerable differentiation. Many citizens might choose to become freedom fighters when basic rights are challenged, but very few would choose to bomb a hospital, skyjack a planeload of innocents, or terrorize an entire citizenry as a selected choice of their freedom fight.

I prefer Benjamin Netanyahu's definition of terrorism. Netanyahu cuts away the rhetoric and really gets to the issues involved. Netanyahu is the brother of the only Israeli soldier killed at Entebbe. He was also the Israeli

Ambassador to the United Nations. His definition was adopted in 1978 at a Jerusalem-sponsored international terrorism seminar. "Terrorism," he says, "is the deliberate and systematic murder, maiming, and menacing of the innocent to inspire fear for political ends."[1] Netanyahu stresses that innocent people are going to be killed in any conflict or war.

> What distinguishes terrorism is the willful and calculated choice of innocents as targets. Guerrillas, for instance, are not terrorists. They are irregular soldiers who wage war on regular military forces, secret police agencies and governmental counter-insurgency police units. Guerrillas do not prefer civilian targets. They do not consciously select civilian victims.
>
> Actually guerrillas are the exact opposite of terrorists. While [guerrillas] put themselves against far-superior combatants, terrorists [will] choose to attack weak and defenseless civilians: old men, women, children—anyone in fact except soldiers, if they can avoid it.
>
> Civilians, then, are the key to the terrorists strategy. They kill civilians, and more often than not, they hide behind them—hoping that the prospect of more innocent deaths will help them escape retribution.[2]

## ■ THE CONTEMPORARY DEFINITION OF TERRORISM

The word *terrorism* became popular during the 1790s of revolutionary France, when it was used to describe what is now known as the *Jacobin excesses.* The aristocracy was executed or escaped to involuntary exile during this era in order to survive. Many of the middle class were also persecuted.

Terror or terrorism is based on the Latin verbs *terrere* and *deterre.* Terrere means to cause to tremble. Deterre means to frighten. These word forms are now quite adequate to describe the ubiquitous phenomenon of this generation as well. Terrorism, then, is a form of intimidation designed to influence politics and government behavior.

Terrorism, though, has a purpose beyond the immediate act. A rapist or a robber may terrorize as the victim is intimidated. All of the fear and terror of dying, being raped, or being injured is going to be present in the assault. But that is the end of it. The terrorist, however, wants the enigma; he wants to create publicity. Terrorists create a worldwide, center-stage media event. The choreography of the event is controlled by the terrorists, but the audience quite often governs whether there will be an encore.

Terrorism has no precise or widely accepted definition, even though everyone seems to really "know what it is." A loose or generic description will almost always include "violence for political effect or impact." Terrorism is also a form of surrogate warfare; it is a very cheap way to fight without actually going to war. Third-world terrorism, with a very limited budget, can still influence a virtual superpower and tie up vast resources of manpower and equipment.

Some cynics even describe terrorism as entertainment. The actions of M-19, the IRA, the KKK, or Sendero Luminoso are also symbolic forms of entertainment to a watching audience. Terroristic incidents are "as diverting as the adventures of the Scarlet Pimpernel, Zorro, or the Lone Ranger and Tonto."[3] Many terrorists attempt to capitalize on a Robin Hood mystique.

In third-world countries, especially in oppressive political regimes, terroristic activities may be silently applauded as terrorists succeed in making government forces appear as failures and in diverting security and police forces at leisure. This is especially true in environments where government corruption is obvious or in those cases where the government is quite casual in abusing its powers and in denying basic human rights to the citizenry.

In some instances, terrorist groups will become totally estranged from the community. This occurred in Argentina and in El Salvador after many businesses closed. The work force was alienated from the terrorists and held the terrorists responsible for the loss of their jobs.

# ■ THE INDIVIDUAL TERRORIST

In defining a terrorist as an individual, there are also many distinct problems. Many personal traits are commonly shared by the ordinary citizen and the terrorist. Some deviants are obviously deviant. A bum or a vagrant is not clean and is dressed in ragged, unkempt clothing. A drunk may stagger as he walks, be profane in his language, and have a florid complexion. The homosexual or the transvestite may be quite obvious in his or her behavior. But the terrorist, his description, and even the acts that define his role, is much more difficult to define.

The terrorist commits acts that are designed to frighten or to induce a state of terror. Unlike the criminal, whose purposes often create fear as well, the terrorist has significant political aspirations. She wants to force change on governments, economies, and on society. Her acts of terror are designed to have consequences beyond the criminal act itself.

# ■ AN UNDERSTANDING

Terrorism is difficult to understand. Quite often its goals and objectives are obscured by the intensity of the violence. Terrorism, however, is not mindless violence. The terrorist action may be incredibly destructive and evil, but the events are generally very well-planned, well-rehearsed, and well-executed. Terrorism is often a grandiose display of power and military skill. It often underscores the weaknesses and vulnerability of a government and its institutions. Terrorists see the world as a stage on which to show the world their problems, their intentions, and their fantasies

A Shiite skyjacking, a South Mollucan train hi-jacking, an Iranian or Libyan assassination, may come into perspective when examined and analyzed. Terrorism is a means to an end, not an end in itself. It has real goals and definite objectives.

## ■ KINDS OF TERRORISM

There are many kinds of terrorism. In terms of activities, there are two kinds of terrorism. The first kind of terrorism is *discriminate terrorism*. Discriminate terrorism is always easier to understand. Discriminate terrorists attack their enemies. The Irish Republican Army's attack on a British Army Hostel is understandable, an example of an enemy striking at an obvious enemy. All of the victims are combatants or potential combatants.

The second kind of terrorism, *indiscriminate terrorism*, is more difficult to comprehend. People are attacked indiscriminately. Casual shoppers on a city street, children in an orphanage, or a planeload of travelers may be perceived to be legitimate targets. Although they have nothing to do with the event being protested, because they are present, they are defined as legitimate targets by indiscriminate terrorists.

Other kinds of terrorism include right-wing terrorism, which is usually a reactionary and pro-government activity, but not necessarily so, and left-wing terrorism, which generally emanates from the intellectual community and is fostered by the desire to change the economy. There are also special-interest groups that address only one social problem. Animal-rights activists in the U.S. have bombed animal research laboratories and abortion advocates and clinics have been attacked by violent men and women willing to use terroristic-style violence to address their cause.

Some terrorists stay in their region; some travel over international boundaries to commit their activities and are called *international terrorists* or *transnational terrorists*. There are also *state-terrorists* (the state, the police, and the military) who use despicable tactics to maintain order in their environment—they use levels of force and violence that are unacceptable to society.

Many terrorists are *nationalists*. They simply want a state, a territory, or country returned and given the name or description used in history. The Palestinian irredentist seeks to recover the land and adjacent regions once controlled by his people. Some of these people are referred to as *separatists* by the media. They want to set aside what they perceive to be theirs or having once belonged to their people.

# ■ WHAT DO TERRORISTS DO?

A risk analysis and assessment needs to be completed so that you know what you may confront. Terrorists have a big agenda, but very rarely do they use an extensive violence agenda. You must know the agenda associated with the area in which you are traveling or working.

> Terrorists act with a limited tactical repertoire. Bombings alone account for roughly half of all terroristic incidents. Six basic tactics comprise 95% of the total: bombings, assassinations, armed assaults, kidnappings, barricade and hostage situations and hijackings. No terrorist group uses all of them. [At the present time], approximately one-third of all terrorist incidents involve hostages.[4]

Knowing that more than 51% of all terrorist events involve bombings and more than one-third of all terrorist activities involve hostage-takings shows the primary risks. The expatriate *must* learn the methods appropriate to living in a bomb-oriented and kidnapping environment.

# ■ IS TERRORISM LIKELY TO AFFECT AMERICANS LIVING OVERSEAS?

"Many Americans living overseas have packed their bags and returned to the U.S.A. or have resigned themselves to a life of calculated risk."[5] The perception that all Americans are rich and powerful influences our rate of victimization, especially in developing nations. The belief that America is capricious in influencing the politics of the world and of supporting unacceptable dictatorships is also another reason that individual Americans are targeted all over the world. These beliefs encourage terrorists to target Americans because they are Americans.

Susanna Purnell of the Rand Corporation completed a study on American businesses abroad. She found that very few businesses leave a terrorism-ridden environment. "Businessmen with overseas investments generally agree that terrorism is simply another risk they must contend with, just as they live with war and violence."[6]

The few businesses that withdrew from these environments left because of long-term economic considerations, rather than terrorism or the threat of kidnapping. The exception to this international standard occurred in El Salvador in the 1970s and Argentina in the late 1960s and early 1970s.

While there is not a general exodus from troubled lands, there still is room for concern for the business traveller. The reason for this concern is that terrorism *is* increasing. There has been a general increase in terrorism during the 1980s. In 1988, the U.S. State Department Report, *Patterns of*

*Global Terrorism: 1988,* shows that there was an increase in fatalities from 1987.[7] However, there was a decline in 1989 and 1990. How long will the decline continue? Is there a slow-down caused by the hundreds of arrests of terrorists? One 1983 Rand report indicates that there was a 68% increase in the amount of terroristic activity against ordinary citizens in a 10-year period.[8]

It is interesting to note that the families of businesspeople living in the U.S. have a more escalated stress level than their family member actually living in the troubled land. Terrorism, like crime, fire, and traffic accidents is something the public gets used to. Actually, the total amount of terroristic violence has been quite small compared to crime, fire, theft, robbery, rape, lightning, or traffic accidents.

## ■ WHO IS A TERRORIST?

Obviously, no one is born a terrorist. Activists do not become terrorists overnight. Most terrorists would not even agree that they are terrorists, but would advocate that they are freedom fighters. Perhaps they would answer to the term *revolutionary;* very few would accept the constraints of the terrorist label.

The terrorist accepts a new way of life when he joins a revolutionary movement. He is indoctrinated with the precepts of the organization. Investigators have often studied the indoctrination systems used by cults and cult-like religious organizations, and have discovered that the terrorist is indoctrinated in a way very similar to the cult member. The convert is given a new status, that of a knight or warrior. He is given something to do, something he perceives to be noble and commendable.

Dr. Richard Clutterbuck of Cambridge University has a 1% theory that relates to terrorism. Dr. Clutterbuck retired as a General from the British Army and his viewpoint is enhanced, perhaps, because of his experiences. He feels that most people, anywhere in the world, do not have the emotional stamina to become involved in violent confrontations. Dr. Clutterbuck stated,

> In practice, there is invariably a mixture and a large proportion of the people, usually a majority, have no wish to get involved and will conform to the dictates of either side if expressed by a man with a gun. Probably a fair average is that only one percent of people feel strongly enough to wish to risk their own lives in support of either the guerrillas or the government. Another ten percent may have sufficient preference to follow the lead of the activists on either side, while as many as eighty percent will do their utmost to keep themselves and their families out of the battle.[9]

Thoughtful observers of all societies have been searching for the truth that could be used to predict both the incidence of terrorism and the traits of individuals that indicate terrorism or pre-terroristic activity. Criminologists have searched for pre-criminal indicators as well. While there are likenesses between the common criminal and the terrorist, there are also substantial differences. The crime of an ordinary criminal is not intended to have consequences beyond the criminal act. The criminal steals to get money or items that can be used for monetary gain. The terrorist, however, wants to change the society, the economic system, or the government.

Occasionally, an intelligence analyst can make interpretations from the goals a terrorist group claims as its own. There are several goals that are usually stated by terrorist groups.

1. The need and desire to receive popular recognition while educating society about the philosophy and objectives of the terrorist group.
2. To obtain official recognition from the government.
3. To broaden their base of power.
4. Undermine the prestige and morale of those in government.
5. Cause a leader to overreact and to lose prestige.[10]

American society regards the terrorist essentially as a complete deviate, a person who is neither shaped by nor in contact with social reality. The traits of the terrorist may also be shared with others of a nation or cultural community. There were only a few South Mollucan terrorists, but many South Mollucans desired to return to their homeland. The same thing is true of the Armenian terrorists in this country or the Afghan freedom fighters being protected by the political policies of the United States Government.

Generally, terroristic motivation can be divided into several types. The terrorism used by most groups is ordinarily based on nationalistic interests, ethnic minority motivations, or economic interests. Motivation concerns land and power more than any other interest.

## ■ A TERRORIST-TRAIT PROFILE

It is very difficult to develop a trait-profile index. The number of skilled terrorists operating in one area at any particular time is usually very small and the groups tend to be comprised of the dedicated, hard-core cadre with a number of relatively peripheral followers. These profiles also indicate that the norms are elusive. There is no such thing as a "typical terrorist." However, the airline industry has been very successful in screening skyjackers through the use of profiles.

In searching the literature for norms and likenesses, I found the following data:

- Terrorists often come from upper-middle class and upper-class families. In Germany, 36% of those arrested came from families in the higher socioeconomic status. Only 23% of those arrested came from families with a lower socioeconomic status.[11]
- Terrorists have a better-quality education than the population as a whole. In Germany, at least 36% were graduates or enrolled in the University at the time of their arrest. The vast majority of terrorists in the University have studied in the humanities or in other non-technical fields.[12] Terrorists are violent intellectuals.
- At the time of their terroristic activities, 20% had a profession, 10% were self-employed, and 26% were employed in more marginal positions.[13]
- In contrast to the guerilla who operates from the forest or the jungle, the terrorist "is, in the main, reared in an urban environment."[14]
- Sixty-seven percent of all terrorists are single; 20% are married; 13% are divorced or separated.
- Only 26% of all captive terrorists have been convicted of previous offenses; 15% have been arrested for street crimes; 11% have been convicted of previous political offenses.
- The age of a terrorist is very young—61% are between the ages of 21 and 30; 18% are under 21; and 21% are more than 30 years old.[15]
- Eighty-five percent of all terrorists are male and 15% are female.[16]

Exceptions to age are found in the PLO and the Baader-Meinhoff constituency. The PLO recruits youngsters of 12-14[17]; the average age for the Baader-Meinhoff group is 31.[18] While only 15% of terrorists worldwide are women, the figure, in Germany, is as high as 40% of the total terrorist population.[19]

The fundamental truth that we find in examining the life of the terrorist is that he is willing to make a complete commitment of his life-style and his life to the cause he espouses. He is willing to flirt with death or to take inordinate chances with his life. The terrorist might be called a *risk-seeker* as opposed to a *risk-taker*. One of the reasons that most terrorists are young is that the career of the terrorist is generally not a very long one.

# ■ ARE TERRORISTS CRAZY?

Some authorities believe that terrorists are crazy or at least psychologically and legally insane. The reports of psychiatrists and psychologists who have had the opportunity to study imprisoned terrorists is contradictory, however. They do not find insanity among terrorists. They have found some support for the insanity theory among assassins who acted alone, but the terrorist organization requires a lot of real discipline and the ability to cooperate with others. People with deep emotional maladjustments just cannot cope with the discipline of a terroristic organization. Also, psychotics have difficulty in keeping their minds on a single subject at any given time. Since most terrorist operations involve a lot of planning and multiple rehearsals, the psychotic would most likely be unable to accept the regimen.

Many terrorists are strongly trained in their ideology and the indoctrination technique is quite similar to those used by cult leaders and teachers within cults. The indoctrination methods occur whether one is a member of the PLO, the KKK, the JDL, or the Baader-Meinhoff Gang. These indoctrination methods were all prescribed by Mao Tse-tung in the Communist Revolution. Some terrorist groups also recruit in a fashion similar to the Moonies or Charles Dedrich's Synanon.

Even though there is strong evidence that most terrorists are not insane, this diagnosis is certainly not an indicator that there are no pathological tendencies or that there are no delusions. One psychiatrist who has studied terrorism reports that there is a "commonality of delusion"[20] between terrorism groups, no matter what their location in the world. These delusions are as follows:

- Delusions of persecution—the group is convinced that it is under serious and dangerous attack. [In many cases this is not true at all, although in others it may be the truth.]
- Delusions of grandeur—A Holy mission or some other type of supreme value is vested in the group by its members.
- Delusions of wish fulfillment.[20] [A situation where fantasy and mythology surround the ideological founder of their movement.]

The delusions of grandeur a terrorist may feel generally include many forms of self-delusion, such as the following:

- Belief that great hordes of people are ready to support them in their violence.
- Belief in their own self-perpetuating propaganda.
- Overestimation of their own strength.
- Overestimation of their own appeal.
- Underestimation of their own weaknesses.
- Belief in the imminency of their own victory.[21]

Terrorists have normal personality characteristics—they want to be liked, accepted, and secure in maintaining a group of friends. They want to have an identity and to have status in that role. While many terrorists may not have a strong sense of family, the young revolutionary may have a strong ethnocentric identity in becoming someone special, someone who fights for freedom or for a bold, new, and better social order. In belonging to this group, the revolutionary matters to someone and has a status never before attained. He has a strong sense of identity to a purpose, a task, and a cause. These revolutionaries do not want to return to the relationships they once shared because those relationships did not satisfy them.

Some terrorists appear entirely amoral in view of the results of their violent onslaught. They are also perceived as being insane, illogical, unscrupulous, and desperate. Yet we find that some terrorists do have definable moral standards. In the Philippines, the New Peoples Army has a very high moral expectation; adulterers are executed. The NPA wants its membership to be more moral and ethical than Christians in the Protestant and Catholic communities of the Philippines.

Society must also realize that terrorists, too, have a political constituency that must be satisfied. In 1988, one Indian tribe pledged a fight to the death if their missionary was expelled from their South American country. In some cases, however, the political constituency expects action and violence. Some audiences may think that the same activities are inhumane and barbaric. However, the terrorist constituency may feel that these activities are justified, appropriate, and morally cleansing. We evaluate the terrorist and the constituency he serves by the quality and intensity of his activities.

Look not to the ghettos and barrios of the indigenous population for the terrorist, rather look at the universities, the colleges, and the business schools. Look at the political scientist and the historian. Look at those who have endured little, if any discomforts or disadvantages. They will be the leaders and the advance party in the coalition of violence.

# ■ REFERENCES

1. Benjamin Netanyahu, *Terrorism: How The West Can Win* (New York: Farrar, Straus and Giroux, 1986), 9.
2. Ibid., 9-10.
3. Yonah Alexander and Seymour Maxwell Finger, *Terrorism: Interdisciplinary Perspectives* (New York: John Jay Press, 1978), 159.
4. Department of Commerce, *Survey of Current Business* (Washington: U.S. Department of Commerce, August 1980), 27.
5. Patrick Collins, *Living in Troubled Lands* (Boulder, Colorado: Paladin Press, 1981), xiii.
6. Susanna Purnell and Eleanor Wainstein of the Rand Corporation, *The Problems of U.S. Businesses Operating Abroad in Terrorist Environments* (Santa Monica, CA: The Rand Corporation, November 1981), 49.
7. U.S. Department of State, *Patterns of Global Terrorism: 1988* (Washington:

Department of State Publication 9705, Office of the Secretary of State, Ambassador-at-Large for Counterterrorism, March 1989), 4.

8. Bonnie Cordes, Bruce Hoffman, Brian Jenkins, Konrad Kellan, Sue Moran, and William Sater. *Trends in International Terrorism, 1982 and 1983* (Santa Monica, CA: Rand Corporation [R-3128-SL], August 1984), vi.

9. Richard Clutterbuck, *Guerrillas and Terrorists* (Chicago: Ohio University Press, 1977), 25.

10. Thomas H. Snitch, "Terrorism and Political Assassinations: A Transnational Assessment, 1968-1980" in Marvin E. Wolfgang's *The Annals of the American Academy of Political and Social Science* (Beverly Hills, CA: Sage Publications, September 1982), 55.

11. Konrad Kellen, *On Terrorists and Terrorism* (Santa Monica, CA: Rand Corporation [N-1942-RC], December 1982), 37.

12. Ibid., 38.

13. Ibid., 38.

14. Yonah Alexander, David Carlton, and Paul Wilkinson, *Terrorism: Theory and Practice* (Boulder: Westview Special Studies in International Terrorism, 1979), 8.

15. Kellen, 38.

16. Arthur E. Gerringer, *Treatise On Terrorism* (Bryn Mawr: Dorrance and Company, 1982).

17. Ibid., 21.

18. Ibid., 21.

19. Ariel Merari, *On Terrorism and Combatting Terrorism* (Frederick, MD: University Publications of America, 1985), 75.

20. C.E. Zoppo, "The Moral Factor in Interstate Politics and International Terrorism", edited by David C. Rappaport and Yonah Alexander, *Rationalization of Terrorism* (Frederick, Maryland: University Publications of America, 1982), 105.

21. Bonnie Cordes, Bruce Hoffman, Brian Jenkins, Konrad Kellen, Sue Moran and William Sater, 49.

# PART II

## ■■ AVOIDING CRIME AND TERRORISM

# 4

## ■ ■ INTRODUCTION TO SECURITY CONCEPTS

The first and foremost security lesson is an important one. This lesson teaches you that *you, alone, are responsible for your own security.* Personal security is a function that can never be fully delegated. Security can be enhanced with technological applications and with trained personnel. A burglar alarm, however, may not work during a power outage or it may be bypassed by a skilled thief. A security guard may fall asleep or be casual or negligent in accomplishing his duties. For these reasons, you should never delegate all of the responsibility for protection of your family, your organization, or yourself.

Delegation is an easy and natural thing when faced with so many issues. Even in the U.S. it is easy to say, "the security patrol employed by my neighborhood association is responsible for securing my neighborhood. Plant security is responsible for assets protection here. My security manager's head will roll if the protection process breaks down. They are responsible for my safety. We haven't had any burglaries, robberies, or rapes reported here since they were employed. I feel safe now!" But the citizen who completely entrusts her safety and security to another is the most vulnerable citizen of all.

Depending on others can cost you your life. Police officers are most often murdered when they are with a partner, not when they are patrolling alone. The officer depends on his partner. The officer feels safer with a partner and does not take as many precautions as is appropriate. The result is often severe injury or even death.

The only person you can truly depend on is yourself! If you are casual about your own security program, you will need to "tighten up" to survive. Ira Lipman, the president of America's third largest security force says, "We can't expect somebody else to take care of our security needs for us. We must handle them ourselves."[1] He urges every citizen to a higher level of personal security responsibility and accountability.

> Personal security is the simple act of protecting yourself from physical harm. It is the accumulation of all the actions you have taken during your lifetime to reduce or eliminate the chances of being assaulted, attacked, beaten, molested, raped or murdered. In fact, you practice personal security to varying

**31**

degrees every day of your life. You have locks on your doors, you avoid high crime rate areas and you are careful of strangers. . . . All of these are basic and elementary techniques of personal security. To a large degree, you take these steps in order to protect yourself from the threat of violence.[2]

Good security is the only answer to a world rife with crime and terror. It is a very positive approach to a negative problem. If you understand that almost all crimes can be prevented, you can learn to survive. While you will not delegate your personal security to others, you should listen to the advice of security professionals.

Terrorists use certain implementation techniques. If you are aware of them and terrorists' mode of operation, you can behave appropriately. You can avoid a hostage situation and save your own life and the lives of others.

Personal security is even more important where police action and crime prevention standards are unacceptable. The poor police standards in many areas of the world compound the difficulty for most westerners. We delegate most crime prevention responsibilities to our police authorities and to our security staffs. Many westerners believe that crime prevention, crime avoidance, and crime solutions are up to police officers, not themselves.

## ■ FOUR KEYS TO CRIME AND TERROR

Any criminal or terroristic attack has four distinguishable stages. There is always surveillance, an invitation, a confrontation, and an assault. If you can understand these four stages, your chances of avoiding an incident are greatly increased and may well save your life.

The deliberating criminal or terrorist surreptitiously observes his potential victim during the surveillance stage. He carefully scrutinizes his target's activities to detect any security deficiency. Intelligence files seized during arrests show that terrorists all over the world plan their actions carefully— as do many thieves, serial killers, and rapists. They decide who they will target next. They then place that person under surveillance and plot their target's daily activities.

Surveillance may be constant or it may be intermittent. The British Ambassador to Uruguay, Sir Geoffrey Jackson, felt that a couple who picnicked at a park across the street from his home were, in fact, surveillants. He also noticed the same motor scooter each day as he commuted to the Embassy. He later discovered that the scooter, with different passengers on board each day, had cut his driver off and made him stop on occasion and slow down on others. The surveillants wanted to see how his driver would respond in an emergency.

Ambassador Jackson later wished that he had acted on his concern; he spent 9 months as a Tupamaro hostage, because he did not react to his feelings. He should have reported the surveillance to Uruguayan Police authorities. A report should be made as soon as surveillance is spotted. By being aware and observant, you can protect yourself. You will be forewarned of an impending crisis and can respond in an appropriate manner.

The invitation stage develops as criminals or terrorists physically approach their victim. The invitation stage is when your vigilance will be repaid in a thousand ways. It is at this stage that you can evade capture and assault, and escape harm.

During the invitation stage, the victim will be distracted or stopped. A rapist, a mugger, or a kidnapper may approach the intended victim with a simple question, "May I get some directions, please?" You may be asked for change or for a match. This stage is entered innocently, as asking for directions, change, or a light for a cigarette are acceptable social exchanges. But to stop, for even a moment, opens the door for criminal activity. You are vulnerable even if you slow down; you are very susceptible to victimization if you stop. But if you never slow down at all, you will thwart the response. This action will throw off the criminal's timing. Avoiding the "stop" may create an environment in which you will not be victimized.

Sometimes, the stop will be "baited" while you are driving. Most men will stop on a rural road to help a woman with a flat tire or who appears to be having difficulty with her vehicle. But the attractive young girl or even the mature matron, may be a terrorist or a thief. Her accomplices may be lying out of sight with their weapons. If you stop, the trap will be sprung.

You cannot afford to stop in a dangerous land. This does not mean that you will never render aid; it simply means that you will find an alternative method of helping. Perhaps you can be the Good Samaritan by paying a mechanic at the next town to go back and help the stranded motorist. Call an ambulance or the police if there seems to be some other problem. Remember, it is very easy to create a vehicular accident scene. Three or four men simply roll an old car over on its side and another feigns unconsciousness in front of the car.

If you stop, the trap is sprung. Do not take an unnecessary risk in a dangerous environment. If the area is known for its guerilla, criminal, or terrorist activity, then be especially careful. Avoid any ruse! Think like a thief! Think like a terrorist! If you have not been observant, you may now be a real victim as you enter the confrontation stage.

In some incidents, the last three stages occur simultaneously. The norm, however, includes a time separation between the last three stages. If you have been watchful or observant, you have already walked away from the stranger who asked directions. If he was a criminal or a terrorist, he is already out of synchronization and the criminal or terrorist plan may be aborted.

The assault is the last stage. During the assault stage, especially if the assailant has a weapon, resistance is foolhardy and possibly even fatal. Many criminals or terrorists will do anything necessary to subdue their victims.

## ■ STAY ALERT

Watch for surveillance, be wary of an invitation, and stay alert, even when you are with friends. If you are walking to your car, approach it as if it were an armed fortress. Have your car keys in your hand, with the door key extended. Be ready to minimize your vulnerability between the time you walk to your car and get in it. Keep your car locked at all times, whether you are in it or not. When you get in your car, lock it immediately before you start your car.

By having your key already in your hand, you will not be distracted by looking for it in a pocket, purse, or attaché. If you must carry packages, consider locking them in your trunk quickly. If approached by a suspicious person, you can always get in the trunk and lock it behind you.

If you stay alert, you can run, hide, climb a tree or telephone pole, or crawl under a small car and hold on to the axle. Only an accomplished criminal, armed with a gun, could get you out. Even a knife-wielder would have difficulty cutting you as you yelled, moved, and kicked to protect yourself. Yelling may be an advantage. Criminals are wary; they do not want to be identified by others and they do not want to be apprehended.

When outside of your home or office, remember to use space and distance to your advantage. Remain alert; watch for all possible threats. Look frequently to the rear. Don't do this as a paranoid reaction, but as a planned response—a crime prevention tactic. Let this become a part of your daily security repertoire, and a habit within your life-style. Train yourself to be constantly aware of the activities around you.

Concentrate on some current event; daydreaming or philosophical contemplation can be dangerous at the wrong time. A vigilant and observant attitude should become a way of life. Police officers, security agents, and soldiers reflect this attitude. They must, to survive. By walking with your shoulders squared and with an erect bearing, you are lowering the chance that you will become a crime victim. By always looking and *seeing* what you observe, you can avoid victimization.

People who act distracted send subliminal messages to criminals and terrorists. "Here I am, I'll be a good victim." Reading books, listening to a headphone set, sifting through a purse or attaché, and looking at the scenery may be sufficiently distracting to enable a criminal to successfully attack you.

If you are observant, you will see that a street gang is suddenly approaching. You will see that you are about to enter the invitation stage of a criminal event. If you are vigilant, you can walk into the doorway of a store or business, hail a taxi, or run. Some victims step into the street and elude their assailants by running against the flow of traffic. Even on a dangerous street, this alternative is advisable over the risks of attack, robbery, rape, and abduction.

You should also listen to your feelings. If you are suddenly frightened or if someone in particular gives you the creeps, then listen to your feelings and leave the area immediately. Do not ignore these intuitive feelings. Intuition can be a powerful crime-prevention tool. Do not let reasoning or logic talk yourself out of occasional concerns of this nature.

Security is the state or sense of safety. It is freedom not only from actual criminal attack, but from the anxiety or fear of attack. Real security requires a knowledge of criminal actions and the methods used to prevent them. Just as a burglar alarm in a home or business increases the level of security for the inhabitants, training may also increase your personal security. I am less at risk because I know how to act, what to do, and what not to do to avoid criminal crises. If you are trained in how to respond, then you will be more likely to react appropriately in an emergency.

> Personal security is the simple act of protecting yourself from physical harm. . . . It is the thoughtful, realistic, and religiously practiced method by which you attempt to protect yourself from harm. It is the accumulation of all the actions you take, all the defenses you build, and all the methods you employ in order to maintain your personal security. Above all, it is a program of positive action with definite requirements, standards, and goals.
>
> You will need to develop a personal security program of your own which will integrate all your plans, actions, and requirements into a cohesive format that will serve both as a guide and as a measuring stick toward achieving a high degree of personal security. Your ultimate objective should be to develop a program that fully serves your needs and provides the maximum security with a minimum amount of expense or inconvenience.[3]

In developing your personal security program, it is imperative that you plan well. Pay very close attention to the recommendations set forth in the planning and policy-making chapters of this book. It is imperative that you learn as much as possible about the country in which you will be working or traveling. Established expatriates are at a distinct advantage. They know the country, the people, the culture, and the language. All of these advantages can help them avoid crime and terror.

Aside from being aware of crime and constantly on the alert, you will change your crime-avoidance agenda from the one you would use in America. Real crime prevention takes place in an environment where cultural adaptations, norms, customs, and habits are well incorporated in your overall security plan.

Crime prevention is often called *target hardening* in the security trade. A *soft* target is an easy target. An easy burglary is accomplished by slipping in through an unlit and unlocked door or through an open window. A hard burglary is one in which exterior lights are kept on all night, doors and windows are locked, and the home owner has a quality doorframe system and uses a burglar alarm. Decals notifying the potential thief of your security equipment should be displayed on all your doors and windows.

In its simplest form, however, target hardening is a concept. It is a practical philosophy that decreases crime or prevents its occurrence against specific individuals. In the ideal sense, a target-hardened home, office, or individual is simply overlooked as a potential target of crime or terror.

Criminals and terrorists do not change their ways of life. They go on to commit other crimes. The target-hardening method, however, keeps *your* crime from occurring. *Your* crime is deterred when prevention and avoidance methods are accepted as a way of life. The person best equipped to protect you against terrorism and crime is *you*.

# ■ A SOFT TARGET

General James Dozier was a U.S. Army executive assigned to active duty in the North Atlantic Treaty Organization office in Italy. In 1981, General Dozier was captured and held hostage for 42 days. After his successful rescue at a safe house, intelligence documents were obtained on a surveillance that had been conducted against him and several other senior U.S. military personnel. The documents revealed that General Dozier had not been the original intended victim. One of Dozier's bosses had been extensively surveilled over a several-month period. It was decided that this individual was too security conscious, was always well-protected, and used his well-trained VIP protection team. Other targets still senior to General Dozier were likewise scrutinized. These officers, too, were very security conscious. They varied their daily routines. They drove in inconsistent patterns to home and work, and were difficult to surveil. Their security teams were precise and thorough. They looked at street people; took pictures of individuals, automobiles and motorcycles who might be surveilling them; and noted strange license-plate numbers. They were involved in counter-surveillance to determine if vehicular surveillance or stakeouts were posted.

General Dozier, on the other hand, was not a security-conscious individual. He did not observe street people nor vary his schedule. He was quite casual insofar as his own security was concerned, because he believed that higher ranking personnel would be targeted. They were targeted, but their security was so good, that the Red Brigade chose a softer target.

He, as have many other victims, underestimated his enemy and his own vulnerability. He was the highest-ranked soft target available in Italy. When the terrorists want a U.S. or western symbol, they choose the weakest link in the security chain because they want to be successful.

Because of the furor raised over his kidnapping, the Italian government prioritized the investigation. Monumental progress was made in identifying the individual members of the inner circle of the Red Brigade. In fact, the organization was nearly destroyed. But organizations like this go through a period of metamorphosis and transform into a new organization.

General Dozier handled himself well, but was in grave danger throughout this ordeal. The Red Brigade, even though they treated him well, killed many of their hostages in previous incidents. The event could have been avoided entirely, however, through adopting a more security-conscious life-style.

## ■ HOW YOU CAN AVOID CRIME

Crime avoidance must be a way of life. It is based on certain tenets, the most important of which is the power and influence of observation. Keeping up with what is going on in your country is very important and knowledge of your enemy is necessary. When you know how the crime or terror organization acts, how it strikes, at what time it strikes, and at whom it strikes, you can adjust your schedule and your life-style to avoid crime and terror. In addition to observing your environment, street, or strangers in the neighborhood, you should move about at intermittent, sporadic times so that it is difficult to establish firm delineations of your normal schedule.

People who have erratic schedules are using target-hardening techniques. If a terrorist knows where you are and when you will be there, it will be easy to victimize you. Businesspeople normally go to work at a certain time, but terrorists may not want to attack at a time and location when there are many friendly onlookers. If you are traveling to another area, you should try to keep your schedule and route a secret, if possible. The fewer people who know your schedule, the better.

Body language is also a powerful communicator. If you are observant and your body language is assertive (not aggressive), then it is easy for an assailant to observe that you are ready to fight or run. A potential victim who has her head down is an easy victim for anyone. The victim will not even be able to recognize their assailant. But an observant target has seen the perpetrators long before they can approach her. She can take offensive, defensive, or avoidance postures.

There are other target-hardening techniques. More than 50% of all terroristic events involve bombs. You should know that the biggest danger in an explosion is not the direct blast (although the blast can kill you), but glass fragments and debris. Stay away from large windows in dangerous environments. If car bombs are the standard operating procedure in your environment, walk as far away from parked vehicles as physically possible. Think safety, think precaution, think avoidance, and think about security. Then act and react in a safety and crime-avoidance mode. Know the danger and avoid it.

## ■ ARE YOU A SOFT TARGET?

It may be that you do not believe that you would be a target for terrorists. Certainly there are government officials, diplomats, military attachés, intelligence attachés, and wealthy executives living in the country you serve. They are probably higher-risk targets than you. You may, however, be the softest target in the area. Those other targets may have VIP protection provided by the U.S. Government, the host government, or private security personnel. They may have professionally designed intrusion alarm systems in their homes, radio-telephones in their automobiles, and security officers at their residences. They may have armor-plated sedans at their disposal and may live unpredictably, insofar as their schedules are concerned.

Are you a softer target than they? Are you the only American living in your neighborhood? Are you the only westerner living there? Are you the only person of your race living in your area? If you answer "yes" to any of these questions, you must become a hard target.

How can you become a harder target? Do what you can to develop personal relationships with nationals in an effort to encourage friendships. This *bonding* with nationals will help you in your work, travels, and may also save your life. Overseas travelers do not always enjoy preferred relationships in the communities in which they live or visit. Many of them never master the predominant language or the dialects, and many never learn about cultural idiosyncrasies. The wealthiest of these people live in closed, well-guarded communities. They rarely interact, as they cannot communicate with the average person on the street.

Natives and national friends can be of tremendous assistance to those who bond with others. They can warn you about crime and criminals, and of guerrillas and insurrection. They can save your life. Terrorists are more likely to attack *ugly* Americans. An ugly American is rude, arrogant, and culturally insensitive. He or she treats locals as if they were of a lesser-servant class. A well-liked or a respected person making a vital social or economic contribution to the area is not as likely to be targeted unless anti-development terror is taking place in your country. When street people like you, they will warn you and help you.

# ■ REFERENCES

1. Ira A. Lipman, *How to Protect Yourself from Crime* (New York: Avon Books, 1981), xxiv.
2. Patrick Collins, *Living in Troubled Lands* (Boulder, CO: Paladin Press, 1983), 3.
3. Ibid., 3.

# 5

## ■■ AVOIDING CRIME IN THE STREET AND AT HOME

Americans are inundated with crime-related information. We hear about robbery, murder, burglary, and rape every day. We read about it in newspapers, see it on the television, and hear reports as we listen to the radio. We almost become impervious to it. Crime is like disease; it is *there!* We hear about it so often that many citizens believe that nothing can really be done about it. We expect crime to happen, especially in the ghetto or barrio, but we do not expect it in our neighborhood and we do not think that crimes will be perpetrated against ourselves, in spite of the statistics that indicate otherwise. We think crime happens to someone else.

> All of us are personally affected by crime. The most important thing you can do to avoid crime is to learn to be aware of who and what are around you. Develop a healthy alertness, but not an unhealthy paranoia about what is going on. If you were taking a stroll through a jungle, you would avoid stepping in quicksand, and if you could, you should try to avoid equally unpleasant experiences in the city. Yet I marvel at the number of people who, after waiting for the pedestrian light to change in their favor, step off the curb without first looking to see if traffic is approaching. They walk smack into trouble without ever seeing it in advance.[1]

## ■ HISTORICAL APPROACHES TO CRIME CONTROL

Primitive man banded together in family groups to protect clan members, tools, and surplus food. Watchmen kept vigil for marauding bands of warring tribesmen. Hills, environmental cul de sacs, and islands have always been used to enhance safety. Many families built cottages on stilts over the water, so that their homes could only be approached by swimming. Early American Indians built cliff dwellings and used caves as these positions were easily defended. Early village dwellers built walls around the village and used single, large entrances for caravans and very small openings for individuals. Emergency exits were very narrow and sometimes only 3 to 4 feet high. A grown warrior could enter it slowly, but would be bent over and in a vulnerable position if he entered a wall through such a door. Defenders inside the walled community could easily kill attacker after attacker in this advantageous position. Sometimes moats surrounded fortress walls as well.

Even the early highway right-of-way laws were designed based on crime-prevention techniques. Today, we think of broad spaces near highways as being safety zones. We can spot a child, a dog, or a large animal before it enters the thoroughfare. The early right-of-way laws, however, were devised to thwart highway robbery. Trees that grew over the road were cut down so that a thief could not drop down and ambush his target. The cleared spaces kept thieves a reasonable distance away from you. You had the opportunity to prepare by drawing a sword or taking evasive action if you were attacked.

The concept of the King's Peace developed in England and the Frank Pledge system evolved in France. Under these programs, a village received a crime tax to replace the valuables a merchant lost during a theft in their village. The *posseos commitatus* (posse) policy was also established and required all eligible men in good physical condition to help apprehend thieves and violent men and women.

The King's Peace statute required every man to carry a weapon at all times. Also, if a citizen saw a crime being committed, he cried out that it was occurring. This crime alert was required by law and was called a *hue and cry*. Shirkers were actually branded with a *C* on their foreheads. The *C* stood for the word *coward*. Crime control was considered everybody's business.

## ■ CRIME PREVENTION IS YOUR RESPONSIBILITY

Today, many citizens around the world somehow feel that law enforcement and crime prevention is police business. When I was younger, I changed careers from police officer to security professional. As a police detective, I dealt with crimes that had already been committed. It was my job to investigate, solve the crime, and make an arrest of the perpetrators. As a security professional, however, I can create an environment in which crimes are not likely to occur. I create an environment in which crime control and crime prevention are everybody's business.

It is unrealistic, irresponsible, and naive for an individual to believe that law enforcement authorities or even your own security service will be available to resolve or intervene when you need them for *your* crime.

Public law enforcement is a relatively new profession. While watchmen have existed for hundreds of years, the modern police agency is modeled after the 1829 innovation of England's Sir Robert Peel—the London Metropolitan Police Department. In many societies, policing is merely a job. The uniform is worn by poorly selected, uninformed, and untrained citizens—who carry guns. We cannot depend on a person of this caliber for our lives or for our safety.

Even with the more than 450,000 public police officers and 630,000 private security guards in the United States, this country must have daily citizen involvement to maintain safety in dangerous neighborhoods. If you do not have that involvement, you are not safe or secure.

You can make a difference if you commit yourself to a crime-avoidance life-style. Obey crime-prevention and crime-avoidance rules. Accept the responsibility for your own security. A good personal security program, coupled with a good community or a building security program is a prophylaxis against stress and fear. Good security does not have to be elaborate, expensive, or time-consuming. Crime prevention should be your best habit.

> Keep your mind and eyes on what you are doing and where you are going. Watch for trouble and stay away from it. If you see people fighting on the street, avoid walking near them. If people are arguing, mind your own business. Avoid being jostled. That's a favorite ploy pickpockets use to create a distraction, but it may also mean you are not paying enough attention to what's going on around you. If you can't see what is ahead of you as you are walking, be extremely cautious and be prepared for what *might* be ahead of you.
>
> Look like you know what you are doing and where you are going, and have complete control of yourself and your environment. Walk confidently and directly, at a steady pace, and be alert and aware of your surroundings and the people around you. Do not walk with your hands in your pockets— you will appear to be less than prepared for danger—and don't carry things in your hands if you can avoid it, unless these things are going to be used as a weapon to defend yourself. If you get into trouble, seek help. If you think you are being followed by another person on foot, walk quickly to where there are people and, if it is night, lights.[2]

## ■ ENVIRONMENTAL PROTECTION

Today, citizens around the world use some of the ancient physical security options with a contemporary slant. A home may have a 20-foot high solid brick wall around it in Lima, Bogata, Quito, Manila, or Beirut. It may be topped off with embedded glass, barbed wire arrangements, or concertina wire (made with stainless steel razor blades). In addition to historical methods you may also adapt modern technology to your needs. Alarm systems may be in place which react to weight, pressure, window openings, door openings, or invisible light beams to announce that private space is being violated.

Private watchmen and bodyguards may be employed by many households or neighborhoods. Many expatriate families of modest means still help pay their neighborhood watchman and expect crime to be curtailed in and around their homes and property.

As electronic equipment continues to be developed, its cost has lowered. Many families can now afford burglar alarms for their homes and automobiles. However, if you cannot afford this equipment, you can ensure that you have quality exterior doorframe systems in your home.

The doorframe system is something that can be built by anyone moving into a new home, apartment, or office. Before the drywall is in place, install a few pieces of 2x4-foot lumber to remarkably strengthen the traditionally weak point of entry into your home or office.

For about $5 you can purchase a doorframe that cannot be easily jammed, spread, or jacked open. Some thieves use a small car jack, place it in the doorframe along with a short piece of lumber, and then spread the doorframe open. A thief does not have to pick a lock, he just jacks the door open until it can be pushed in.

If you have a good doorframe, however, this is not likely to happen. To have a satisfactory doorframe system, you also need a good, solid core or steel door on which hinges are exposed only on the inside of the house, a quality lock-and-knob system, and a reinforced doorframe. If you do not reinforce your doorframe, a $100 lock and a $300 door are wasted money. A hollow-core door is also a cheap substitute for a quality door and only appears secure. A hollow-core door is built like a picture frame—all of its strength is in the circumference. The center is veneered plywood with a cardboard insulator. A young person can easily punch his fist through a cheap, hollow-core door. A criminal can do the same, then just reach around, unbolt the lock or turn the doorknob, and be inside your home in 3 seconds or less. A cheap, hollow-core door provides no security at all.

While a reinforced doorframe *can* be broken, it requires considerable strength, additional time, and would make a lot of noise. Most burglars would not want to make that much of a commotion.

You can also build a *safe room* in your own home that has quality exterior doors and a quality exterior doorframe system. If you have a telephone or radio transceiver in your safe room, you can call for outside aid.

## ■ CURTAIL YOUR CRIME

In dangerous communities, citizens must never let down their guard. You must never let any stranger get close enough to you to compromise your security. Do not walk alone through dangerous areas. Robberies, assaults, rape, and murder increase when security carelessness and inattention is obvious.

Crime rates increase when citizens do not help each other fight crime.

Neighborhood watch programs work in any country. The only necessary "weapon" is a telephone or a radio. Unfortunately, most westerners don't do anything at all to protect themselves from crime and terror.

> One criminologist studied the kidnappings of Americans in Latin America from 1970 through 1985. He found 781 reported kidnappings. Although the victims knew that Americans were being targeted, in the vast majority of cases they failed to exercise even elementary security practices.[3]
>
> If security practices had been utilized, it is possible that abductions would probably have been cut by 50 to 70 percent.[4]

## ■ AVOIDANCE PREPARATION

Being prepared can save your life. You are ready to react. Failing to prepare can be exceptionally costly. Preparation is more than a state of mind; it is a statement of the ability to respond.[5]

> In our scheme of things, a security function is one requiring the person entrusted with it to make some predetermined action to safeguard life or property by interposing authority or some other capability to that end. While varying amounts of discretion will be conferred upon those entrusted with such functions, there is always the clearly defined sense of mission or purpose. It is clear what has to be done even though there may be room for argument as to how this has to be accomplished.[6]

It is clear what has to be done to protect our property, our families and our businesses. We must make it harder for others to victimize us. Target hardening is not expensive or necessarily time-consuming. It is a simple method designed to avoid, deter, and prevent crime. Whether one lives in a protected subdivision surrounded by walls and guardposts or in a high-crime inner city area, target hardening can work for you. Through target hardening you can substantially increase your own safety and that of your family anywhere in the world. The methods are compelling, common-sense approaches to crime and terror.

Two generations of Americans were exposed to a tried and true prevention tactic. Smokey the Bear appeared on television every Saturday morning and said, "Remember children, only *you* can prevent forest fires." Similarly, a terrorism philosopher would say, "Remember folks, only you can prevent your own victimization."

## ■ THE AUTHOR'S RESEARCH

More than 100 expatriates have informed me that they are more afraid of the legitimate police and military agencies of their adopted country than they are of revolutionaries. Some businesspeople are frequently stopped at legitimate police roadblocks by the authorities and later at illegal road-blocks by revolutionaries. The reports I have received from Latin America, Africa, and the Philippines indicate that the guerrillas are more polite and less confrontational than the police and military units of those same countries.

Businesspeople, diplomats, and military personnel are often ill-prepared for a terroristic incident. The average westerner expects wealthy nationals, high-level governmental leaders, members of the diplomatic corps, members of the military and police services, or wealthy expatriate business-people to be targeted by terrorists.

Businesspeople are also of symbolic value and, therefore, are very important to terrorist groups. The expatriate's nationality may be more important to the terrorist than possible extortion. An expatriate may also become a high-risk target overnight because her home government made a political or economic decision that is unpopular in a particular locale.

A high-risk person in a high-risk area can learn to function with relative safety. Strong security considerations should impact every person living in such an environment.

## ■ REFERENCES

1. Jay R. Dixon, *Personal Protection and Security* (Chicago: Nelson-Hall Publishers, 1985), 94.
2. Dixon, 98.
3. Charles Russell, "Kidnapping As a Terrorist Tactic," *Terrorism and Personal Protection*, edited by Brian Jenkins (Boston: Butterworth Publishers, 1982), 19.
4. Arthur J. Alexander, "An Economic Analysis of Security, Recovery, and Compensation in Terrorist Kidnappings," *Terrorism and Personal Protection*, edited by Brian Jenkins (Boston: Butterworth Publishers, 1982), 187.
5. H.H.A. Cooper and Lawrence J. Redlinger, *Catching Spies: Principles and Practices of Counter Espionage* (Boulder, CO: Paladin Press, 1988), 365-366.
6. Ibid., 373-374.

# 6

## ■■ DEVELOPING SUCCESSFUL TRAVEL STRATEGIES

You may be much more secure than you think. The security executive can extrapolate a lot of good intelligence material to help you maintain your personal security through a security strategy. The material is easily available, but must be obtained from many separate sources. The time to begin a successful travel strategy is during the planning stage of your trip. Without proper planning, you are inviting trouble. Terrorism is an international threat that requires advance knowledge of the victim, his itinerary, and his location. Travel security can limit your risk. Some corporations keep travel-safety intelligence data on a full-time basis.

If you are a frequent traveler, you should begin developing a security life-style that promotes safe travel. The techniques for avoiding crime and terror are quite similar, although the tactics will vary somewhat as you seek to avoid all unnecessary risk. Almost all of the precautions recommended involve common-sense approaches.

> American travelers should be increasingly alert to the hazards of overseas travel and should prepare for them ahead of time. It is safer to travel abroad than it is to walk down a city street at night in the U.S.[1]

British terrorism researcher, Dr. Richard Clutterbuck, says that "only one air traveler per 500,000 is ever inconvenienced by terror and the 499,999 who reach their destinations will then be statistically more at risk than they were on the aircraft.[2] In general, safety statistics favor travel over staying at home.

When you travel to unknown areas, be sure to run a security check. Do not assume anything. You should not assume that your destination is safe or secure just because you have not read about any activity pertaining to crime or terrorism in that country. Recall that in dictatorships, the news is controlled. If the dictator does not want a full disclosure of news relating to violence in his country, the article is suppressed.

The dictator also allows western newsmen into his country, or he rejects their visa application. Those who are there may be more interested in remaining (alive) than in correctly reporting events that are difficult to officially document. In some cases, a country may have had a "bad press" for a long time, yet be relatively safe now.

The U.S. State Department Emergency Hotline can tell you whether or not an area is safe. They can tell you about the types of crimes that are affecting westerners. Discover any specific threats to your safety or security. Research this well. You may be able to plan your itinerary in such a way that you will avoid the major hot spots and minimize difficulty.

Review the more prominent newspapers for several weeks before you depart. *The Washington Post, The New York Times, The Miami Herald,* and *The Los Angeles Times* are probably all available at your local library. Note any incidents in the countries scheduled on your itinerary. Start your own file of crime and terroristic incidents in the countries you will be visiting. Get friends, relatives, and co-workers to help you cover the best news magazines, television, radio news commentaries, and newspapers.

Become a member of Compuserve, a private news compendium of all major papers. The electronic bulletin board of the U.S. State Department's Overseas Security Advisory Council (OSAC) is also computer-accessible by all U.S. companies. Punch in your membership number and obtain the data you need.

Take the time to discover if there will be any holiday events during your trip. Many travelers and expatriates have inadvertently failed the security timing test. Choose dates that are not likely to coincide with national liberation days or civil unrest. OSAC keeps up with the major anniversary dates of most countries.

> All in all, your chances of being the target of any kind of terrorist attack are probably about equal to your chances of winning $1,000,000 the first time you buy a lottery ticket. But when you travel abroad, put your common sense in gear. . . . Many people travel extensively and never have a problem. I think that's because they use common sense and travel defensively.[3]

## ■ PRE-FLIGHT ARRANGEMENTS

Make all travel arrangements as soon as possible. In foreign countries, try to limit the number of personnel who have specific knowledge of your agenda. If an organization representative purchases your tickets, she can set them aside without your name appearing on the ticket until later. Your ticket will still be secured.

A trusted travel representative can ensure your confidentiality. Change travel agencies if any agent ever releases information regarding your tickets.

Instead of using a travel agency, you might wish to use a ticket agent at the airline you prefer. Choose your airline based on its safety record and ground security procedures, not because it offers the cheapest tickets or the best in-flight meals.

In some countries, the primary flights out of the country are on a national airline. Sometimes these airlines are more expensive, but the extra cost is worth it. The best safety and security records are held by American, British, German, and Israeli airlines.

Some travelers pick airlines with the widest seats or with the best cuisine. Do not make this mistake! Choose security over expense in dangerous areas of the world, at especially provocative locations, or during dangerous times. I repeat, "In dangerous times and at dangerous locations, you should choose the airline with the best safety and security record." Do not ignore airlines that have been victimized by terrorists on previous occasions. Several of these airlines provide the very best security, precisely because they are so often targeted.

There are many activities that you can accomplish to increase your own travel security, aside from choosing your airline. You can choose the airports through which you enter or leave a country. Avoid dangerous airports if you have the option. The Athens, Greece, air terminal was known as the most dangerous airport in the world for several consecutive years. The security there was either too lax or nonexistent.

Sometimes travelers fly to other cities and drive to their primary destination, rather than flying into a dangerous airport. You can make these decisions intelligently if you have consulted with the State Department Hotline and watched the news services.

You can also choose your travel dates, and travel times. Did you know that terrorists do not like to seize night flights? Choose a wide-bodied jet; they are less likely to be hijacked. You can also select direct flights. Flights with stopovers are riskier. Direct flights reduce terrorist access to your plane.

Also, ensure that your family and co-workers do not give out your travel itinerary to callers. At the office, let another staff member take your calls while you are out of the country. Should an emergency arise, a family member or a co-worker can locate you and deliver a message, rather than release your itinerary to a stranger.

There are many other actions that you can take to increase your own travel security. The key to good security is to maintain a low profile. Far too many travelers unwittingly advertize their own vulnerabilities. Choose the quality and appearance of your luggage, the uniqueness of luggage identification tags, and your seat.

> Genuine leather luggage, for instance, may impress your friends, but it also tips off potential adversaries even before you board a plane. It is a signal that you are a person of means. Consequently, you are a symbolic target as well as a good commodity to ransom.[4]

Choose where you will wait prior to your departure from the terminal. Reconfirm all of your reservations immediately prior to leaving for the airport. If your flight is delayed, do not spend additional and unnecessary time waiting at the air terminal.

Each of the judgments you make, relative to these choices, is of critical importance. Choose to keep your luggage locked at all times, except when going through Customs. This activity minimizes pilferage and limits the possibility that bombs or smuggled goods will be concealed in your luggage by someone else.

> Carry no information which, given its content, could endanger you, your company, or other company members and avoid carrying information that could be misinterpreted. When documents are not essential for travel within a country, leave them in your hotel vault or your company's custody.[5]

These decisions may set the stage for survival or death should a crisis occur. Judgments that may seem rather inconsequential at home are of critical importance somewhere else. Obey the rules and you will have a happier, more peaceful, less stressful visit.

## ■ WHAT TO WEAR

Dress comfortably. Do not dress extravagantly or with apparent pretention. A man wearing an unbuttoned sport shirt, gold necklace, heavy gold bracelet, and a Rolex Watch is a crime looking for a place to happen. Check the preferred wardrobe of the country you are visiting. In some countries, the recommended dress is a suit and tie rather than more casual clothing.

A former airline Chief of Security states that men in business suits have not been selected for abuse by hijackers, but that those in casual clothing have often been abused. He emphasizes that it is often preferable to wear a business suit while in transit to, in, or around terrorist hot spots. The suit can save your life! Normally, men who are picked as scapegoats are those whose status is degraded, not the well-dressed businessman. Many terrorists are financed by business benefactors. They never want to bite the hand that feeds them, so they pick someone without status to be their symbolic victim. Businessmen who degrade their own status do so at their own peril.

Women, too, should be very careful. You can meet the cultural norms for foreigners or expatriates without dressing in an ostentatious manner. Leave all your good, quality jewelry at home. If your costume jewelry is so nice that an uninformed criminal might mistake it for the real thing— leave it at home. Do not be mugged for an unimportant accessory. The risk is not worth the benefit. If you feel that you must wear these accessories, conceal your watch, rings, earrings, and necklaces and put them on immediately prior to entering your destination.

Do not wear jewelry imprinted with Jewish markings or the Hebrew language. The display of Israeli or Jewish emblems is not a good security practice in areas with large Islamic populations. The wearing of these ornaments raises the probability that you will be a crime or terrorist victim.

## ■ LUGGAGE

Your luggage should not be pretentious. Even if quality luggage is a gift from loved ones, think twice about using it if you are traveling to a high-crime area or to an environment frequented by terrorists. You would not want to be randomly selected as a symbolic target merely because it appeared that you were wealthy, influential, or powerful.

Some authorities recommend that you take only the absolute minimal essentials with you when you travel. Then you can carry all of your luggage on the plane. This practice not only prevents the loss of your luggage by the airline, but it is also a good security practice. You do not look prosperous with one old bag. Too much luggage may also restrict your activities should you need to run or defend yourself. Too much luggage labels you as a victim. The criminal knows he can steal more from you because you obviously have more to steal.

The philosophy behind crime avoidance or crime prevention is to circumvent criminal selection. Avoid looking like a person of wealth, status, or power. Leather luggage is expensive and attractive, but it attracts the attention of criminals and terrorists as well.

Your luggage identification tag should be selected with care. Many civic clubs sell distinctive tags with room for personal identifiers on one side. Do not use them. Rotary, Kiwanis, Pilot, and Civitan Clubs are all western-based and perceived as capitalistic identifiers. You may be perceived as having wealth or influence just because of this identification. The American Express cardholder may now purchase an exquisitely embossed luggage tag, but the American Express Card and luggage tag is a symbol of a western value system. To a westerner, it simply shows that you have reasonable credit and are, at least, a member of the middle class. To people of other lands, it may symbolize all the negatives associated with wealth.

Some organizations use plastic sealing devices to enclose business cards. These are then conveniently attached to the luggage handle. However, by using these, you may give terrorists or criminals more information than is necessary. Your luggage tag should be used only to identify your luggage if it is lost in-transit by an airline.

Dr. Stephen Sloan, a prominent terrorist researcher and the author of several books on terrorism, recommends that you "buy luggage tags that cover your identification cards. They can be read only if they are actually opened. That brings attention to anyone but yourself."[6]

You should also tape or mark your name and address on the inside of each piece of luggage. *Travel Safety: Don't Be A Target,* published by Uniquest Publications, recommends that you also tape your itinerary inside your luggage in order to claim your luggage.

You should be very careful about all of your descriptors. Make sure that the name on your luggage tag matches the name on your airline tickets to expedite the retrieval of the luggage if it is lost. The following are examples of my own address identifiers used over the years:

Dr. Chester L. Quarles, Vice President
Contingency Preparation Consultants
Southern Regional Office
Post Office Box One
Tula, Mississippi 38675
USA

Dr. Chester L. Quarles, Director
Mississippi Bureau of Narcotics
Mississippi State Government
State Office Building
Jackson, Mississippi 39205
USA

Professor Chester Quarles
Criminal Justice Programs
The University of Mississippi
University, MS 38677
USA

Chester L. Quarles
Highway 331, Box 227-C
Oxford, MS 38655
USA

The last address is preferable. The purpose of the luggage tag is to identify the owner in case the luggage is lost. The other address identifiers only serve to impress a baggage handler or a bellhop at the hotel. They do not need to know that I have a Doctorate degree, am a college professor and researcher, or have served as a crisis management consultant. I do not want them to think that I have status, wealth, influence, or political power. To give a greater impression is to increase your chances of victimization. If you have a title, such as Doctor, Chairman, President, or Director, you may wish to drop it for luggage identification purposes.

If you use a plastic-enclosed business card for your luggage identifier, look at it carefully. What does the card suggest or symbolize if a terrorist or street criminal were to read it? If there are status indicators on the card (such as being associated in *any* way with a Fortune 500 company), take the card off your luggage and use another method for luggage identification.

All of these recommendations apply to your briefcase as well. Leave your business cards, business brochures, and corporate letterhead in your checked luggage. Do not leave easily identifiable data around for a terrorist to review. Keep your glasses and necessary medicines in your attaché or in any other carry-on bags. You will need these even if your checked luggage is misplaced or stolen.

Many tourists collect luggage decals to indicate their travels. This is *not* a good idea. It shows frequent travel and implies wealth and status. Keep your luggage clean and free from all attention-gathering items. You do not want your luggage to attract anyone's attention for any reason.

# ■ AT THE AIRPORT

In dangerous areas, it is best to say goodbye to your family at the air terminal entrance. Leave your family at the drive-by unless there is concern about whether your flight will depart.

The greatest danger at an air terminal is from a bombing. More than 50% of all terrorist attacks involve some form of bombing. Be especially careful around unattended luggage or packages. Do not stand near glass panels.

There have also been multiple assassinations with machine guns at air terminals. At Heathrow Field, assassins fired at unidentified passengers waiting on an El Al (Israeli Airlines) flight. These tourists, including men, women, and children, were massacred in just a few moments. Leave your family at the terminal entrance.

Avoid leaving your car at the airport if this is at all possible. Some thieves check tag registrations, determine that your home is unoccupied, and burglarize your home. Your car is also subject to burglary. It is best to take a taxi cab or other public transportation to the airport.

The safest areas of an airline terminal are on the flight deck. The most dangerous areas are ticket counters, waiting areas near ticket counters, luggage carousels, and rest rooms. Bombs have been placed near these locations in many instances. Do not browse in the main terminal area. Duty-free shops are usually in the secured areas. Go there. Check your luggage in at the ticket or luggage counter, walk through the guarded metal detectors, and go immediately to your boarding area. This part of the air terminal is more secure than the area open to the general public as there has already been a security screening of passengers and carry-on luggage. At this point, travelers have been separated from the rest of the airport population.

> By going immediately to the boarding area, you will also avoid another breed of criminal. Pickpockets are still alive and well. They still ply their trade. Even in the U.S., pickpockets are increasing. In the four year period between 1976 and 1980 the rate of these crimes increased nearly 50% in the United States.[7]
>
> Airport pickpockets often watch ticket counters or newspaper stands to determine the location of the mark's wallet. They work the ticket lines and the area just outside the security screening area. It is the departing passengers, who still have money in their pockets, that they're after.[8]

As you wait, look around and become familiar with all exits, including emergency exits. Do not just concentrate on knowing about exits that go down into the street or in front of the terminal, but exits that may lead down under the airport terminal or in other directions as well.[9]

The best place to sit or stand is near columns or posts that are supportive structures for the building. Do not go to sleep while waiting to board your plane. Remain alert to all that is going on around you.

Should there be an evacuation alert of the air terminal, stay in the center of the crowd. Don't panic and race out in front or drag too far behind. We're talking survival and a crowd around you like secret service agents surrounding the President provides a buffer between you and danger.

If there is a commotion or problem anywhere, quietly get out fast—but do not run or you'll be suspect. There is nothing you can do, so don't let your curiosity get you involved. There could be secondary attacks. Keep a low profile.[10]

## ■ ENTERING THE AIRPLANE

The plane is normally the safest place to be. Enter the plane as soon as you are allowed. If you have planned your trip properly, you should have ordered your tickets well in advance. Check the seating charts for the aircraft in which you will be traveling. Try to secure a window seat away from bulkheads or emergency exits. Do not accept first-class seating. Even though you should not sit by an emergency window, ascertain these locations so that you will know where to exit in the event of a crash or forced landing. Check your overhead luggage area for unaccompanied packages or bags. Also, check under your seat and in the pocket behind the seat in front of you. Slip your hand behind your seat to ensure that nothing out of the ordinary is in the cover of your seat. Never accept a sealed package from a casual acquaintance or from a stranger.

The smaller, narrow-body jet airliners like the Boeing 727 or 737 are hijackers' favorite targets. They are a smaller plane, which makes it easier to control the passengers.

The hijackers seem to avoid the large, wide-bodies like Boeing 747s, the McDonnell Douglas DC-10s, Airbus A-300, and Lockheed L-1011s. None had been hijacked overseas since 1970, until Pan Am Flight 73 was hijacked in Karachi, Pakistan, in September 1986.

The problem with hijacking a large wide-bodied airliner is there are just too many people to control for the small number of hijackers usually on board. The more hijackers who try to get aboard, the greater the risk of being detected, so they have been sticking to the smaller airplanes.[11]

If you are a man and are traveling with your family, let your wife or children sit in the seats closest to the aisle and take a window seat. The greatest danger for a western man is to be pistol-whipped. If you are not convenient to the aisle, the chances for this event happening are significantly decreased. If you do not create a disturbance or attract attention, you will probably not be harmed in any way.

Women are rarely abused during skyjacking attempts. Children, too, are normally left alone. Abusing women and children is not good politics for most terrorist causes. Most terrorists abuse men only. The exceptional cases in which women have been harmed normally involved hysteria and extreme emotion. In a very few cases, women were harmed merely because they were Jewish or had Jewish sounding names. Only in the rarest of incidences were they killed. I have never documented a rape during or immediately after a skyjacking, although one stewardess received a marriage proposal in the last Beirut hijacking.

Read and reread skyjacking materials carefully. This knowledge can save your life. Avoid all first-class passenger seating when traveling to, through, or near troubled lands. Terrorists usually use the first class section as a command center. The first-class passengers are more likely to be abused than the other passengers. First class passengers nearly always lose their seats and, at the other extreme, are also most likely to lose their lives.

Take only the materials you need with you. Keep your passport on your person, as well as your ticket and boarding pass. Everything else, except perhaps some reading material, should be placed in your checked luggage.

## ■ EXITING THE AIRPLANE

Once you have left the airplane, the secure area of the airport is the safest place to be. In many less efficient airports, you will probably have a long wait before you can clear the passport station and Customs. Wait in the secure section of the air terminal until you are sure your luggage has been unloaded before you cross into the less-secure areas of the air terminal. As you wait, remember the instructions about explosions and glass damage. After you retrieve your luggage, stay clear of the carousel and all lockers. Past incidents show that bombs are placed in incoming luggage or in lockers.

If someone you have never met is there to pick you up, develop a code system. Having someone hold up a placard with your name on it is not a secure method. I, personally, will not leave the airport with someone that I cannot speak to or understand. If a native driver arrives, I will call my office or friends to affirm that the person claiming to be my driver is who he claims to be. Use a code or an organizational membership pin that is easily recognizable by all members of your organization. This prevents any unauthorized intrusion to the organization's transportation process.

## ■ PUBLIC CONVEYANCE

If you use the taxi system, watch the pick-up line. Try to pick a later-model taxi that appears to be in good mechanical condition. Make sure that *you* pick your cab and driver. Do not allow a driver to pick you. As you check out the cab, make sure that the door handles are present on each door. Do not get into a cab that you cannot get out of without assistance. Avoid the use of the gypsy taxi system entirely (drivers who are not licensed taxi drivers that come to international terminals and offer rides for cash. The gypsy taxis are untracable and much more likely to mug and rob or steal your luggage). Many countries require taxi driver registration. The registration form is normally placed in a prominent location. Compare the picture on the registration with the face of the driver before fully committing yourself to the ride.

If you have carefully prepared for your trip, the embassy may have already informed you of particular cab companies that use preferred, pre-employment methods to filter thieves, procurers, or revolutionaries from their midst. If several members of your organization are traveling together, jot down the license-plate numbers and police registration number of each taxi in your procession. Insist that the vehicles travel together. This highly visible gesture is very target hardening and may prevent your robbery, abduction, or murder.

The American Society for Industrial Security suggests that you never request cabs by phone in an international situation. You should also tell your taxi driver not to to pick up any other passengers. If the cab is not metered, agree on a price before entering the cab and before allowing the driver to put your luggage in his trunk. Many drivers will leave the scene after a price battle, with all of your luggage still in the trunk of the cab.

If you are familiar with the area or know a safe route, insist that the driver travel the roads and streets you have selected. This will keep you out of any high crime-rate areas and is another effective target-hardening method.

In some countries, the presence of an air conditioner in the cab is advisable. This ensures that not only are the doors locked, but all the windows are rolled up too. Thieves and revolutionaries have been known to throw tear gas, feces, or snakes into a slightly cracked window in order to get the passengers or driver out of the car. Air conditioning prevents this from occurring.

Never let your arm hang out of the window of a cab. Many young thieves make a good living cutting watches and bracelets off of wrists at intersections.

Avoid the public bus system within most inner cities. The jeepneys of the Philippines, for instance, are often robbed. Even though a visitor is not likely to be robbed on a public conveyance, she may be followed from the vehicle for a purse-snatching, mugging, rape, or murder.

If you are traveling by bus across country, be aware that many preferred transportation companies offer special first-class buses or first-class seats on buses. The rule recommended for air transportation does not apply to bus transportation. Pay for a more comfortable seat on a bus; it will normally be located nearer the driver and is safer as well. You are less likely to be bothered or molested in any way.

The same passenger status rules on airplanes do not apply on cross-country trains. First-class seating is advised here, as well. It is safer. The first-class cars are normally separated from other passenger sections. The first-class attendants are normally more security conscious than in other locations of the same train. If there is not a first-class section, pick a compartment occupied by several other passengers. Do not sit in an unoccupied compartment by choice.

## ■ HOTEL ACCOMMODATIONS

Think about security when you plan your local room arrangements. Do not check into a room that is accessible from the ground floor. Check into a western hotel or a hotel with a western security approach. Remember that commercial lodging is designed primarily for sleeping and not for protection. The best-protected hotels in which I have stayed were in Colombia and in the Philippines. Security personnel were permanently stationed on each floor. At the Philippine Plaza Hotel in Manila, there were 16 ground-floor security people on duty during each shift. This did not include bellhops and other service personnel.

Many travelers are not aware that there may be fire or smoke-inhalation danger in accepting a room higher than the 7th floor. This is true even in America. There are two 13-story dormitories in my town in North Mississippi. We are more than 80 miles from a fire department that has a ladder long enough to reach these floors. In developing nations, there may not be a fire truck of that capacity in the whole country.

I recommend that you attempt to register for rooms on the 4th, 5th, 6th, or 7th levels. You are not only removed from street crime, but you are better protected in the event of a fire. You may choose to take a portable smoke detector with you.

As you exit the elevator or stairway when first entering your floor, check the location of all emergency exits and the placement of fire extinguishers.

I always carry a small, but powerful, flashlight operated by two fresh alkaline batteries in case the lights go out or in case there should be a fire.

If you take the elevator up to your room and discover any security threat between you and your room, reassess the room locale.

> Do not enter your room if there are suspicious people in the hallway. Walk back to the elevator. [Perhaps you can even walk quickly down a stairway if the elevator is not available.] Go to the hotel clerk and report your suspicions to the manager. [12]

When you reenter your room, lock the door and alternative locking mechanisms. Ensure that doors to adjoining rooms are locked from your side. Never open your door for people you do not know or services you have not requested. Report any security discrepancies to the hotel management immediately. Remember, you are responsible for your own safety.

If there is a lot of violence in the city you are visiting, you may want to consider an inside room, or at least a room that does not face the more prominent thoroughfares. If you do not have a choice over the location of your room, remember that bombing is the primary danger from the street. Avoid using your balcony or frequent exposure to the windows of your room. In explosion-prone environments, leave all your curtains and sun screens closed. This will help catch some of the glass fragments and will minimize damage to you and your room in the event of a bombing. Do not go to your window if you hear shooting or an explosion. Do not work adjacent to your hotel window.

While staying in your hotel, be careful and remember all security rules. Lock your doors and keep the deadbolt and security chain in place at all times that you are in the room. Look out the peephole if someone knocks. If you feel uncomfortable in any way, call the front desk before admitting service personnel, maids, bellhops, or even security officers. Many robberies have occurred because a victim trusted a hotel uniform. Some travelers carry portable lock devices that are commercially produced to doubly secure hotel room doors.

> Be careful about the company you keep in an elevator. If you do not like the looks of someone in the elevator or if you are already in when they get in, get out. Many elevators are equipped with alarm buttons for use in an emergency. Do not hesitate to push one if you are in trouble. [13]

When you leave your room, minimize pilferage by locking your bags. A skilled thief can open your bags, but the average thief cannot. Also, hotel employees prone to stealing from guests are unlikely to force open your bag, although they may take advantage of any opportunity to steal unsecured valuables. Do not use a travel lock to secure furniture drawers;

this simply pinpoints the location of your valuables. This type of device only discourages maids and service personnel who have legitimate access to your room.

If you have anything really valuable with you when you travel, take it with you or secure it in the hotel safe. Some travelers, both male and female, use money belts or wallets suspended from shoulder harnesses to store their valuables.

## ■ DINING

Carefully choose the restaurants in which you dine. Avoid streetside tables in dangerous lands. Sit inside any selected restaurant or cafe. Try not to sit near the front door or at the more prominent tables.

> Sit as far as you can from the main entrance and close to alternate emergency exits since most bomb placements or throw sites are right inside the front door. Notice where the emergency exits are.[14]

## ■ AUTOMOBILE TRAVEL

Remember that a high percentage (more than 80%) of kidnapping and assassination attempts occur while the victim is in his automobile. When selecting a car to lease or own, there are some important choices to make. Pick a car that is in good condition and one that has good tires and sound brakes. You will want a vehicle with plenty of power as you may need to accelerate quickly to get out of trouble. Pick a crashworthy car model commonly seen in your new location that is plainly painted without special emblems or licence plates. Select a vehicle with a low profile. An extravagant cherry-red sedan does not meet the criteria for a low profile. Avoid any vehicle that makes you look like a rich American.

> It is important to remember that your primary goal is to achieve a level of security that will make you a difficult target, and this encourages the potential attacker to select an easier target. Your ability to evade, escape, or defeat an attack is secondary to that goal.[15]

When selecting a car, get one that has air conditioning. You do not want your windows down in heavy traffic, at stop lights, or when you are stopped at major intersections. The car should be in good condition and should have seat belts, interior locks, power brakes, and power steering. It is preferable to get a vehicle that enables you to open your trunk and hood from inside the car. You will also want a locked gas cap, as well.

Some vehicles are reinforced at their bumpers. This is highly desirable. You can have it done if it has not yet been accomplished. If someone tries to force you off the road, you can avoid the attempt without extensive damage to your car. A strong, heavy-duty shock absorber will also help avoid problems and give greater vehicular stability during any evasive techniques.

You must also have good tires with a well-defined tread. The tires need to be constantly inflated to their proper pressure. Some security consultants recommend running tires with 38–40 pounds of air pressure. You will feel more bumps, but the car will have greater stability, especially if you must jump a curb or turn off a road onto another surface.

Security authorities almost always recommend that you keep your fuel tank at least half full. Then you are not likely to run out of gas at a time when you need it the most.

As you drive, keep a reasonable distance between cars to the front and rear, if at all possible. This will prevent you from being boxed in. You can always drive forward, change lanes, or back up to avoid a kidnapping situation, although this may be very difficult to accomplish in dangerous lands where the driving-courteously-and-defensively codes may be non-existent. Plan when and where you will drive to increase the probability that your trip will be safe and successful.

When exiting from your car, carefully observe the immediate area. Do you feel threatened? Is there anything that is "just not quite right" about what you observe? Can you see any strangers? Do you observe any strange vehicles? Is your sixth sense warning you that something is just not right? If the answer to any of those questions is "yes," drive away and return some other time. Your intuition may well save your life.

If you have parked your car for any period of time, check it over carefully before starting it. Do you see anything different? Is there a handprint or a smudge on your car? Has any mud or dirt been knocked off from the underside of your car? Do you see any wire or wire clips under your vehicle? Remember to look for indications that someone has placed a bomb there. Is there a suspicious object underneath your car? If you do not check it out, you will never know until it is too late.

## ■ REFERENCES

1. Peter Savage, *The Safe Travel Book: A Guide for the International Traveler* (Lexington, MA: D.C. Heath's Lexington Division, 1988), xix.
2. Richard Clutterbuck, *Kidnap, Hijack, and Extortion: The Response* (New York: Saint Martins Press, 1987), 79.
3. Jay R. Dixon, *Personal Protection and Security* (Chicago, Nelson-Hall Publishers, 1985), 71.

4. Steve Sloan, *The Pocket Guide to Safe Travel* (Chicago: Contemporary Books, 1986), 23.
5. Herbert L. Saunders, William J. Mulligan, and Richard E. Keiser, *The American Hostage: To Be or Not To Be* (Vienna, VA: Virginal Cardinal Publications, 1988), 8.
6. Sloan, 24.
7. Dixon, 64.
8. Ibid., 65.
9. Dan McKinnon, *Everything You Need to Know Before You're Hijacked* (San Diego, CA: House of Hits Publishing, 1986), 49.
10. Ibid., 49–50.
11. Ibid., 37.
12. Dixon, 70.
13. Ibid., 50.
14. Saunders, Mulligan, and Keiser, 11.
15. Patrick Collins, *Living in Troubled Lands* (Boulder, CO: Paladin Publishers, 1982), 82.

# PART III

## ■■ SURVIVING CRIME AND TERRORISM

# 7

# ■■ KIDNAPPING

Interviews with more than 500 international residents and frequent travelers, and the results of questionnaires referencing safety and security matters reveal that kidnapping is the security threat feared most.[1] Murder, rape, robbery, burglary, and larceny take 2nd, 3rd, 4th, 5th, and 6th place, respectively, after the concern of kidnapping.

In environments in which kidnapping is virtually a daily occurrence, the threat disrupts the lives of overseas personnel and their families in a very significant way. More than 30% of all terrorist attacks are directed against Americans.[2] Approximately one-third of all terrorist incidents now involve hostages,[3] and the amount and frequency of hostage-taking incidents is increasing. In fact, Latin America is the capital of hostage-taking. While the Mid-East holds its captives for longer periods of time, Latin America has 65.1% of all recorded kidnapping incidents since 1970.[4]

One very fortunate aspect of kidnapping is that hostages are *seldom* murdered. Even when demands are not met, execution is rare. As a matter of fact, some 79% of all hostages who were killed perished during rescue attempts.[5] Experience indicates that if a captive does not resist during the assault, he will be more likely to survive. Resistance should never be offered in the face of overwhelming force.

## ■ WHY KIDNAP?

Terrorists seize hostages because they want to draw attention to themselves. They believe that in holding a human life, their power is increased. Their extortion, whether political or financial, is more likely to be successful. Individual targets are normally selected for their symbolic value.

The family or business of a kidnapped person is usually notified promptly, although in some instances the terrorists may wait several weeks to notify anyone. In 1978, one team of terrorism scholars reported that 70% of all kidnappers require ransom payments in half an hour or less, in spite of the fact that few corporations could turn over any currency in that time, except the small amounts held for petty cash.[6] However, extensive periods of silence were noted in the Bruce Olson case of 1988–1989 and in the Roy Libby and Dick Grover case of 1989. The kidnappings of Argentina, El

Salvador, Colombia, and Peru are almost standard daily fare on television newscasts across America.

## ■ WHAT CAN A VICTIM DO?

Any victim is much better off emotionally if he trusts the organization to do everything possible to secure his prompt release. Brian Jenkins discovered that the average stay in terrorist captivity was 38 days.[7] However, there is some indication that the average hostage tenure is increasing. If the victim understands that the usual hostage incident is not a short period, then he will be much more likely to adjust satisfactorily. Certainly it will help the victim if he knows that 98% of all kidnap victims are eventually freed.[8]

The victim should also know that there are rules of etiquette where hostage behavior is concerned. Knowledge of this behavior is beneficial. If you are kidnapped, realize that it is your responsibility to survive. No one will be at a terrorist encampment to advise you how to act. You should comply with the discipline of the encampment.

Resistance is futile in most instances. Occasionally, an opportunity for escape exists. Normally, the escape opportunity opens during the first moments of the abduction. A careful driver or an observant pedestrian about to be targeted may see the danger before it is enacted. This is the time to elude capture, not when someone already has a gun at your head.

It is very risky to resist a hostage-taking encounter. However, for some people it may be more risky not to resist. These personnel would normally be associated with government, military, intelligence, or criminal investigation agencies. The ordinary expatriate or traveler is ill prepared to resist physically, especially when firearms are being displayed and superior force is obvious.

## ■ TRAINING

A traveler or expatriate living in dangerous lands should undertake training to enhance security. You must learn how to survive the stress of a kidnapping encounter. You must learn what to do, what to say, and how to conduct each day's activities. You must also learn what not to do, what not to say, and how not to act. The concept of being a successful victim should be accepted.

## ■ ADVANTAGE

Time is in your favor. As hours and even days and weeks go by, your family and friends may give in emotionally to the stress. However, you must remember that an inverse law exists in hostage contacts—the longer you survive, the greater the likelihood that you will live to walk away from the incident.

## ■ THE STOCKHOLM SYNDROME

The reason that your chances for survival increase is that a bonding (called *introjection*) normally takes place during abductions. Mistreatment could prevent the bonding from occurring, as could disease or infirmity.

Because of an event that took place in Stockholm, Sweden, many psychologists refer to introjection as the *Stockholm Syndrome*. Interestingly enough, the Stockholm Syndrome did not originate from a terroristic encounter. In 1973, a bank robbery was botched in Stockholm. More than 60 customers were in the bank when the criminals used a Swedish K 9mm submachine gun to fire into the plastered walls and ceilings of the bank. Before the criminals could leave with their stolen money, police surrounded the bank and a 131-hour hostage ordeal began.

Ian Erick Olson, the lead armed robber, had many social skills. In fact, many of the victims later noted that he was a "charming gentleman." They also testified in his behalf during his robbery trial. One young female clerk was so smitten with Olson that they were later engaged to be married.

When police negotiators attempted to expedite the release of many of the victims, the *victims* objected, fearing that the police would shoot Olson and his associates. Each of the remaining hostages later visited Olson in prison and developed friendships with the convicts during their visits to the prison.

When the Stockholm crisis was concluded, police officials, psychiatrists, and other mental health care professionals were given a name for this unusual form of crisis-related behavior. The Stockholm Syndrome is now considered to be a normal reaction to the crisis and stress of a major hostage trauma. In fact, many hostage negotiators now hope that it will occur and try to increase the chances for its occurrence. The Stockholm Syndrome is a symbiotic relationship—it is mutually beneficial for the hostage and the hostage-taker. If the hostage negotiator understands the syndrome, he can use the relationship in significant ways.

In another respect, the kidnap victim may have what some psychologists call an *infantile response*, because the victim is dependent on the hostage-taker for liquids, food, and even permission to use restroom facilities. Just as a child depends on its parents for water, milk, nourishment, and hygiene, so does the victim depend on the hostage-taker.

In some hostage situations, the abductors apparently even become surrogate parents. It is hard to view a parent as evil, even when mommy or daddy is sometimes abusive. The terrorist, then, may be viewed as someone whose purposes and philosophy needs to be understood.

As the bonding intensifies, it becomes increasingly difficult for the kidnapper to kill his victim. The kidnapper may have no qualms at all about killing a nameless and faceless person, but it is quite another matter for him to execute a victim he has come to know as an individual or even as a friend.

The bonding process is one that is important to the life of the victim. It can save his life. The hostage should, after the first few hours of captivity, begin a realistic dialogue. "Can I use the restroom?" "I am thirsty; may I have some water?" "This lady's baby needs some milk, may we have some?" These requests are reasonable; they are not confrontational. Terrorists do not want to live for several days with hostages who smell like urine, excrement, or even body odor. Hostages on TWA Flight 847 were even allowed to shower and change clothes at Beirut Airport. Even under the most adverse conditions, reasonable ground rules can be developed between the victim and captor.

Another positive point for a victim and his family and friends to consider during a kidnapping is that assassination is easier to accomplish than a kidnapping. Assassination risks one terrorist, not a group of terrorists. If the kidnappers wanted to kill you, they would take one rifle, one sniper, and one bullet, and shoot you from a position that is relatively safe for the assassin. However, because you were kidnapped, they want you to live. You, too, want to survive, so you must do those things that will help you (and them) succeed. Time is in your favor.

The U.S. Task Force on Disorders and Terrorism recommends that victims attempt to establish dialogue with their captors. However, political discussions should only be initiated by captors. All conversations should be of a nonconfrontational nature. Some authorities recommend a non-communicative stoicism on the part of captives, but this attitude is hotly debated. In a thorough review of the literature, it was found that military personnel, diplomats, business executives, and missionaries were normally communicative with the factions that held them.

If you are being held hostage, it is important not to disturb the development of the bonding process. While bonding is considered to be a pathological transference, it still helps you develop a positive relationship with your captors. The bonding process *must* be left alone. To intrude is to reacquaint yourself with the terror that initiated the pathological transference. Reacquainting yourself with his terror may cause you to initiate dangerous or provocative defenses that may even lead to your death.

# ■ HOW SHOULD YOU ACT WHEN YOU ARE FIRST ABDUCTED?

Kidnap victims are usually mistreated in the initial stage of a confrontation. The psychology of the event is to bring the victim under prompt control. To frighten the victim into submission, verbal abuse and threats to kill are almost universal. It is indeed a frightening occasion. Profanity, as well, is to be expected in many cultures. Once the initial onslaught is over, you can normally expect reasonable treatment if you remain passive. Female victims are rarely raped or sexually abused by terrorists. The greatest inconvenience to women is the total loss of privacy insofar as hygiene and body elimination are concerned since the guards for the women are usually men. The guerilla guards may also be females, watching over the male victims, so this remains a rather universal plight.

Sexual abuse would much more likely occur in a criminal group kidnapping. Terrorists do not usually abuse prisoners in this way. The usual kidnapping occurs to extort money, to demonstrate the power of the subversive group, and to reinforce the public conception of the government as being corrupt and inept. Terrorists gain a tremendous amount of publicity during these operations. The following is an example of one exception to the safety rule for captive females:

> Conflict between the authorities and the victims' families has sometimes produced tragic results in Colombia. The police often keep families under surveillance in hopes of catching the kidnappers. While sometimes this covert activity has succeeded, it also has failed. The police, for example, intercepted the transfer of funds to secure the release of 17-year old Isabel Christina Zuniga Jiménéz. By interfering, the police aborted the payment and the infuriated terrorists—in this case the ELN—murdered the girl after first raping her.[9]

Fear for the family does become a major concern for the expatriate provider. Terrorists, however, generally *do not* target the families of businesspeople. Remember that terrorists rarely murder their hostages. The Jiménéz rape and execution was an exception because the ELN thought the family had double-crossed them. Actually, the military had intervened, seized the ransom, and arrested the courier. *The family acted in good faith,* never realizing that the government was eavesdropping on all family and business telephone calls.

When a hostage is killed, it is quite often the result of some action by authorities. Remember that some authorities focus on capturing or killing terrorists. All governments do not prioritize the life of the hostage. The government's philosophy is extremely important to the business organization that must decide whether to cooperate with the host government or maintain secret negotiations.

Obviously, some police units are more humane than others. Some police units are highly skilled and have many investigative and intelligence resources, while some are not and may be totally inept.

# ■ PLANNING SHOULD PRECEDE KIDNAPPING

People traveling and living in dangerous environments should plan for crime and terrorism-related crises before they occur. Charles Russell, the Senior Analyst for Risks International of Alexandria, Virginia, ran an analysis of 781 kidnap operations between January of 1970 and the end of March 1982. His analysis clearly shows that "in the vast majority of all cases, victims failed to exercise even elementary security practices. Had such practices been allowed, the number of abductions would have been cut by 50 to 70%."[10]

Dr. Frank Ochberg, a psychiatrist of international reputation and the former Director of the Michigan Department of Mental Health says, "individuals should discuss the potential for abduction and the implications of it with [significant] others. One should consider, as concretely as possible, what might happen and the realistic ways of responding to the danger."[11]

Evidence of the value of preparation for potential victims is growing. Banking institutions and other high crime-rate businesses learned, long ago, the value of teaching potential recognition, crime avoidance, and survival techniques. Trained employees are better able to cope. Their training also aids them in the post-incident adjustment process. Employees that are not trained have a tendency to become hysterical and are more frequently traumatized by the experience.

The businessperson or traveler is often ill-prepared for such an incident. They expect some other wealthy American to be held hostage. They expect some other business institution with vast resources and liquid capital to become the next victim. Perhaps, though, terrorists believe that all American-based businesses are quite wealthy and that institutions and organizations buying cars, houses, and airplanes or those that build factories, transportation depots, and retail outlets have bank accounts suitable for the terrorist cause. Perhaps they believe that these institutions, as well as other businesses in their territory, should pay a fixed revolutionary tax each week or month to support their cause and to ensure protection.

The embassy officer is protected by a complex array of information (intelligence), equipment, and protective personnel. U.S. military personnel also take very careful precautions. Only the independent American expatriate who takes a laissez-faire approach to security and the concept of crime prevention remains at high risk.

# ■ BECOME A SUCCESSFUL VICTIM

When a kidnapping occurs, it goes without saying that the captors want the victim to live. The victim is worthless to them, even as a symbolic value, if he is sick, injured, or dead. The few exceptions to this rule have been broadly published in the media. Because the deaths were given such a great amount of media attention, the public accepted these few incidents as the norm, rather than the exception. Should you become a victim, you must always remember to control your emotions during the abduction and in captivity.

## The Regimen: How To Stay Alive

You can be a successful victim by remembering that it is your responsibility to act appropriately. Your actions will greatly influence how you are treated while being held hostage.

Some victims respond to a terroristic encounter in a very hostile manner; they think of themselves as a selected victim and become very angry. The victim who can look at the event as an outsider and philosophize that he or she just got caught up in an unusual set of circumstances will be more likely to adapt to and cope with the captive environment.

Remember, in a terroristic encounter, the rules of war normally accepted by all U.S. servicemen do not apply. There is, quite often, a completely different set of values being demonstrated in the terroristic setting. Soldiers, sailors, and airmen were always told to cooperate by only giving their name, rank, and service number. A victim of a terrorist kidnapping, especially a civilian, must live by another set of rules entirely.

As a kidnap victim, you should maintain your composure and mental health by recalling that most hostage victims survive the ordeal. There are some salient facts that you should recall. A kidnapper, especially one who does not use a mask to maintain his anonymity, will jeopardize his own safety if he releases you, as you can now identify him. Therefore, some kidnap victims propose never to identify any of their captors in police line-ups or mug books.

Bonding and the mechanisms it entails are antithetical to emotional reactions, arguing, debating, or fighting back. All of these responses are what psychologists call *counter-phobic* behavior. Counter-phobic behavior, ''Rambo'' behavior, or macho behavior will get you killed. Once again, it should be stated unequivocally that resistance should *never* be offered in the face of overwhelming force.

Terrorists and even criminal kidnapping gangs are known to make group decisions. The decision to kill you or to allow you to survive may be made by the group member with the fewest scruples and the highest regard for his own freedom. Therefore, you must unobtrusively influence those terrorists closest to you. This should be done as soon as possible; use time wisely.

The hostage should then set out to establish and nurture a bond with the captors. This activity can save your life. It may be your only option because the sponsoring organization may be unwilling to make any concession, offer any compromise, or accede to any ransom demands.

Even when an organization is attempting to establish dialogue to save a hostage's life, the government may be trying to prevent the dialogue from taking place. Some organizations seek to move the negotiations to another country, perhaps even another continent. But this cannot always be accomplished.

The terrorist will elicit compliance with a number of symbolic acts, though the activities may have various consequences. On an international flight, a skyjacker may seize passports. This is often done to identify persons of particular nationalities, races, and religions. Sometimes the hostage-taker will ask to see a military passport or a diplomatic passport. Palestinian terrorists, for instance, sort out people with Jewish-sounding names. Sometimes wristwatches, attachés, wallets, and other personal belongings are also taken. If they are returned, this assists the terrorists in establishing a nice-guy image. Hostage-takers reward the behavior of cooperative victims and penalize the behavior of the uncooperative.

Mayer Nudell and Norman Antokol use the get-rid-of-the-jerk phrase to describe one form of hostage-taking behavior. Anyone who causes the captors trouble or acts uniquely will normally be selected as the first scapegoat, if one is to be used.

The hostage who has been prepared or trained for the ordeal will leave the event a stronger and more vital person. Hostages have reported that all preparations prior to the event were a great help to them throughout the crisis. If you know what is happening and know what to do and what not to do, you will be able to resume a normal life more quickly than those victims who were not prepared.

## The Importance of Building a Relationship

The business executive, who is taken hostage more often, has some strengths on which to build. The very social skills that put her at the top of the organizational pyramid will serve her now. Form friendships; bond with your captors as much as possible. These relationships can be very satisfying. People who are well liked are less likely to be crime or terrorist victims. Among terrorists, it is not popular to mug or terrorize a nice person. Even terrorists prefer to victimize people who have bad reputations and poor community images.

International corporate executives and overseas diplomats do not always enjoy preferred relationships in the communities in which they live. Many never even attempt to master the predominant language and many never learn about the culture and the people. The wealthiest of these people live in closed, protected communities with other wealthy westerners and very wealthy local citizens. They rarely interact as they cannot communicate with the average citizen. They are exclusivists and develop their own subculture, club activities, and after-hours activities. This is not the best attitude to adopt. For your own security, consider alternatives. Learn about the culture; learn to communicate verbally and to read the language of the country in which you work or travel—these gestures may save your life.

## ■ REFERENCES

1. Chester L. Quarles, "Danger Appraisals in Developing Nations," *The Journal of Security Administration* (June 1988) 11(1), 22–43.
2. Brian M. Jenkins, *International Terrorism: The Other World War* (Santa Monica, CA: Rand Corporation, November 1986), 14.
3. Brian M. Jenkins, "Statements About Terrorism", *The Annals of the American Academy of Political and Social Science: International Terrorism* (September 1982), 463 (14).
4. Garardo Capotorto, "How Terrorists Look at Kidnappings," *Terrorism and Personal Protection* (Boston: Butterworth Publishers, 1985), 14.
5. Brian Jenkins, Janera Johnson, and David Ronfeldt, *Numbered Lives: Some Statistical Observations from 77 International Hostage Episodes* (Santa Monica: Rand Corporation (P-5905), July 1977), 27.
6. Paul Fuqua and Jerry V. Wilson, *Terrorism—The Executive's Guide to Survival* (Houston, TX: Gulf Publishing Company, 1978), 125.
7. Brian M. Jenkins, *Hostage Survival: Some Preliminary Observations* (Santa Monica: Rand Corporation (P-5627), April 1976), 9.
8. Leon D. Richardson and Kevin Sinclair, "Negotiations III: The Richardson Negotiations," *Terrorism and Personal Protection* (Boston: Butterworth Publishers, 1985), 279.
9. William F. Sater, "Terrorist Kidnappings in Colombia," *Terrorism and Personal Protection* (Boston: Butterworth Publishers, 1985), 126.
10. Charles Russell, "Kidnapping As a Terrorist Tactic," *Terrorism and Personal Protection* (Boston: Butterworth Publishers, 1985), 18.
11. Brooks McClure, "Hostage Survival," *Terrorism in the Contemporary World* (Westport: Greenwood Press, 1978), 277.

# 8

## ■■ CAPTIVITY SURVIVAL

Assume that you have been held hostage for many days. It appears that you will remain a captive for an extended period of time. Remember that it is *your* responsibility to ensure that you remain in good health. There are many decisions you can make to stay in good shape and many actions you can take to increase the chances of walking away from the episode on your own two feet.

> Once in captivity, your enemy will not be your kidnappers, *it will be your attitude*. Try to control your fear and [your despair]. These two destructive emotions will quickly reduce your ability to resist and maintain your emotional stability.
>
> Constantly remind yourself that your family and company are working for your release. The crisis management team will be working for your release within hours of your kidnapping.[1]

The statistics show that if you are taken hostage, you are *not* likely to escape. Therefore, you will have to prepare yourself to endure captivity.[2]

When you are held captive, you lose all, or most, of your basic human freedoms. You can no longer make normative choices, but you *can* choose survival and good health. Choose to maintain a good mental attitude under the most desperate of circumstances. Elect to exercise every day, even if you are handcuffed or chained. Also, eat all of the food products distributed to you and drink as much water as possible.

Some captives just give up. They lose hope; their faith in God, in their government, in their organizations, in their fellow man just vanishes. They become lethargic and their bodily functions slow down. Not only is this loss of faith not good for their mental health, but it is detrimental to their physical well-being as well. A captive who sits on the ground for great periods of time may experience kidney dysfunctionalism. Your body's toxic wastes will not be properly expelled and toxemia may result. However, toxemia is an avoidable physical condition, if you eat and drink what is offered.

Keep up your strength. Ensure that you could walk out on your own two feet, or escape, if the opportunity exists. You cannot always control when you will be fed, but you can control when you eat. Stockpile food and water in the event that a meal is missed or is inedible.

Many hostages are kept in open, rural areas, but some are held in the city. In an apartment complex, a victim may actually be kept in a tent in the apartment's living area. The tent is used to curtail the victim's observation. If this should happen to you, be comforted by the fact that your captors want you to live. If they intended to kill you, these elaborate precautions would not be necessary.

Some hostages have been kept in old mines, abandoned warehouses, and even in cellars, caves, or dugouts. For a considerable period of time, Sir Geoffrey Jackson was stationed in an underground septic seep adjacent to a factory restroom.

> Time is something that all [of us] are tied to. Suddenly, time, its restrictions and its methods of measurement, have been taken away from you. You must develop some way of keeping track of time. It could be scratches on a wall, notches in a piece of wood, etc. Running your life according to time is a natural human habit and helps bring order to daily life. This will be taken away from you [in captivity]. It is vital to maintain some sort of schedule.[3]

## ■ DAVID JACOBSEN'S SURVIVAL STORY

American University Hospital Administrator David P. Jacobsen was abducted near the entrance of the Beirut-Lebanon Medical Center on May 28, 1985. He was released 17 months later.

Jacobsen was blindfolded for much of the time during his first few months of captivity. He was also chained by his right ankle in a position that did not allow him to complete sit-ups. In spite of the chain, he was able to turn and complete push-ups and leg-lifts. Sometimes he would jog in place when released to use the toilet.

Jacobsen decided to "take just one day—each day, at a time."[4] He would spend time in elaborate fantasies, pretending that he was with his family. He knew he was missing his son's wedding, so he imagined how it would be.

Jacobsen was held with Terry Anderson in Beirut. He also spent time with Thomas Sutherland, the Acting Dean of the School of Agriculture at American University. When alone with Anderson, they were able to talk quietly. These men were held in the room adjacent to Father Lawrence Martin of the Catholic Relief Organization and Reverend Benjamin Weir of the United Presbyterian Church. Later, Father Jenko and Benjamin Weir were also placed in their room.

Humor had a role in helping the "Beirut Five" stay in good mental health. They decided to design a Hostage Survival Kit that every American should carry with them overseas. Since many of the kit items were ridiculous, they really enjoyed themselves. "All of us literally had tears running down our cheeks with laughter."[5]

The captors played some cruel tricks on the Beirut Five. Benjamin Weir was released first. Anderson had been there longer than anyone and he should have been released first. In fact, the captives decided together that they should leave in the order of their arrival. When Father Jenko was released, they were told that they all would be released. They were not. David Jacobsen stated, "I rejoiced for him [Father Jenko], but his release became the catalyst for a series of events that brought some of my darkest days in captivity."[6]

Even as he wrote an article for the *Los Angeles Times Magazine*, Jacobsen stated strong feelings in discussing his ties to Lebanon. At that time, Sutherland and Anderson were still captives. As of this writing, Anderson is still being held. The following are Jacobsen's thoughts about Anderson and Sutherland, his fellow prisoners:

> I'm still in chains until Sutherland and Anderson are out. I don't have nightmares now. I sleep well and exercize hard. I lead a constructive life. But those guys are still heavy on my mind and I can't forget their situation. It was my situation for 17 months and I pray that it won't be theirs much longer.[7]

## ■ BENJAMIN WEIR'S SURVIVAL STORY

Presbyterian Minister Benjamin Weir had served the people of Lebanon for more than 3 decades. When he was first captured by the Hizbollah, he chose not to reveal his knowledge of their language. He chose to speak in English and hoped that they would speak in front of him in their native tongue so that he would receive vital information. Later, an informed Shia told him that they were aware of his language skills. The Hizbollah had quite a dossier on Weir's background and ministry.

Weir made a commitment to himself early during his captivity.

> I felt a mood of challenge rising within me. These men had seized me and thought of themselves as victors, but I would not accept being a victim, even though I might appear submissive and unknowing.
> I hated their denying me my freedom and continuing what I saw as good and worthwhile service. They cut me off from my wife, family, friends, colleagues, and students. It was unjust and wrong, and I would resist as best I could without openly inviting further violence.[8]

In times of depression, Weir stated that he felt "like a dog on a leash." As an evangelical Christian, his faith sustained him. Even his captors gave him reason for hope.

In confronting his own emotions, Weir said that he prayed for patience.

He helped maintain good mental and physical health by practicing "sit-ups, then bicycling on my back, a few back arches, then body twists, squats and stretching exercises."[9]

## ■ DIEGO ASENCIO'S SURVIVAL STORY

U.S. Ambassador Diego Asencio was taken captive in February 1980. Posted in Colombia, Asencio had served some 30 months as the U.S. Ambassador at the time he was seized at a Dominican Embassy reception in Bogota. He was captured and held hostage for 61 days, along with other ambassadors and dignitaries.

Ambassador Asencio wrote *Our Man Is Inside* while recovering from the episode. The following is a small measure of his emotion:

> It is difficult to convey the sense of helplessness that moved like a disease among us, breeding a crippling existential fear. It is difficult to describe the thousand hours of fruitless waiting and the hundreds of dashed hopes. I learned to read pain and disappointment in the faces of my fellow hostages. I learned how to confront fear—my own and others—and how to deal with it.
>
> Looking back, I understand that some of the worst dangers came not from the people who held us at gunpoint, but from those who were ostensibly committed to rescue us.[10]

Diego Asencio stated that "staying alive was my top priority and I was careful not to do or say anything to antagonize [my] keepers."[11] Unfortunately, Asencio quickly learned that there was an informer among the hostages.

The hostages had developed a possible escape plan. After receiving a tip about their escape plan, Commander One (the leader of the M-19 group holding them hostage) cautioned them against trying to escape. Asencio was extremely depressed that there was a traitor among the group.

## ■ DR. CLAUDE FLY'S SURVIVAL STORY

Dr. Claude Fly was determined to come out of captivity in better physical condition than when he went in.

> I exercized twice daily. The six-by-seven area was open to me now, but I could take only two steps forward, three sideward, and two steps back toward the wall—and alternate two-three-two—on and on for hours at a time, until the guards would slip the curtain aside and watch me as if I were some wild animal restlessly pacing its cage. I did deep knee bends, leg and arm exercises,

and, bracing my hands against the outside wall with my feet as far away as would be safe on the slick concrete floor, did push-aways. With these exercizes and deep breathing, I found myself improving. In fact, one of the guards made the remark that I would be a better man for having been in their Tupamaro cell—if and when I was exchanged.[12]

In spite of his commitment to maintaining good health, Dr. Fly had a near-fatal heart attack during his last week in captivity. His captors decided to release him immediately, after he was checked over by a cardiovascular specialist while in captivity. Dr. Fly was released with an accompanying physician at the Hospital Britanica in Montevideo.

## ■ FAUSTO BUCHELLI'S SURVIVAL STORY

Fausto Buchelli was an Equadorian national. He was also an industrial engineer who worked for Hartell Industries and resided in southern California. In 1979, his company temporarily assigned him to a manufacturing facility in El Salvador. Shortly after being sent there, he was kidnapped. Bruce Chapman, another executive of the same company, was abducted at the same time.

Chapman had received contingency training; Buchelli had not. Chapman knew enough to cooperate and was treated very well. Buchelli was rebellious and, therefore, abused. After more than 30 days in captivity, Buchelli was asked to translate Chapman's diary, which had been written in English, into Spanish for the benefit of his captors. Buchelli later wrote,

> I had been jolted many times by unexpected circumstances, and it happened again. I could not believe what I was saying with my own mouth. Bruce Chapman hadn't been in captivity—he had been on vacation! He was being housed in his own room, complete with an operational toilet and a shower. He was given a full pair of pajamas—the right size—and a normal bed to sleep on. He was given three meals a day. In fact, he not only got to eat "real food," but was allowed to select his menu on occasion (including hamburgers and french fries). The kidnappers provided him with many of the creature comforts he requested: cigarettes, liquor, and a radio. He even got to watch the World Series on television! He received tapes and letters from his wife. The only inconvenience he experienced was that he wasn't allowed to leave—he was a captive, technically. The only thing he asked for that he was denied was a woman.[13]

Buchelli, on the other hand, had been abused. He had been struck on the mouth, and his denture bridge was broken and destroyed. He could no longer chew certain foods. He had been stripped naked when he was interrogated, and his wedding band, watch, and another ring were taken.

The sum total of my agonies overwhelmed me. From childhood it had been ingrained in me that strong men do not cry. But with the rash and the tremors came this additional humiliation—an acute emotional sensitivity that triggered weeping spells.[14]

When Buchelli was released after 47 days of captivity, he had to be carried. His period of captivity was very traumatic and his post-traumatic shock disorder was extensive. Buchelli's company was apparently indifferent to the problems he had as a result of his captivity and he did not have a good attitude toward Hartell Industries. He complained until he was discharged.

Buchelli's case is mentioned as a negative example. His ordeal is documented in *Hostage!* Physical and emotional health can deteriorate in a very short time frame, as evidenced by Buchelli and his 47-day captivity. Since many, perhaps most, hostages are now held for longer periods, should you be taken hostage, you should make an effort to maintain good health habits starting with the very first day of captivity.

## ■ INTERROGATION

Interrogation can be a frightening, debilitating, and exhausting process. Study the process carefully. While most interrogations do not include physical abuse, the psychological pressures are extensive. Most hostages are not mistreated, if only because an interrogator needs useful and reliable information, not the information obtained from a mistreated victim.

If you are interrogated in captivity, pause before each question to determine where the question might be leading. There is a second reason for establishing the habit of pausing. People pause on sensitive subjects but not on other subjects. Pausing before each question denies an interrogator the opportunity to find out about what subjects you are sensitive.[15]

You must be very careful in everything you say and do. You must show reasonable respect toward your captors if you wish humane treatment. Often this requires some knowledge of the culture. In Vietnam, many POWs were beaten when they crossed their legs. In our culture, this act has no special connotation—we do it to get comfortable. In an Asian culture, the display of the bottom of the feet is an act of disrespect. The failure to realize this nuance increased the abuse of many Vietnam POWs.

Everything you do, everything you say, your tone of voice, and even your emotions, body movements, and facial expressions are very important.

Question-and-answer sessions are always difficult. A soldier is authorized to give his name, rank, and serial number. He has carefully studied the Code of Military Justice. But what code does a diplomat have? Or a humanitarian worker? Or a missionary? Or a physician?

Ambassador Geoffrey Jackson was interrogated frequently during his 9 months in captivity. He wrote,

> From many books that I have read and plays I have seen, I had an idea of the pressure of interrogation. Yet no account, description, or representation can communicate the depth of weariness and nervous and physical exhaustion which so strange an experience leaves to its participant.[16]

Dr. Claude Fly, U.S. Aid Agronomist to Uruguay, was also interrogated. His captors insisted that he criticize the U.S. Government. He said,

> Several times they [the Tupamaros] tried to get me to condemn the U.S. and to admit that only socialistic and communistic forms of government could meet the needs of the people. I was so exhausted and confused by the barrage of questions and propaganda that, when the ordeal was over, I lay for hours, perspiring and praying on my cot.[17]

Interrogations are intensive, emotionally distracting, and exhausting. If you are captured by a revolutionary organization, or even by common criminals, you will probably be subjected to some form of interrogation. Your captors may simply want to know the approximate monetary value that you represent, so that they know how much of a ransom demand should be made. They may also have a particular interest in information relating to the operation of your business organization.

Common interrogation tactics are fairly standard the world over. The good guy–bad guy routine is frequently used. In this method, one interrogator acts as if he wants to protect you and be your friend and the other interrogator acts like he would like to tear your head off. You receive despicable treatment from one interrogator and comfort, support, and even sympathy from the other, if only you will answer a few questions.

On occasion, an interrogator will accuse you of terrible crimes, knowing all of the accusations are false. But in demonstrating that you did not commit the more heinous offenses, you provide him with a basis for accusing you of lesser matters. In reality, the lesser crimes are the ones in which the interrogator is really interested.

If you are subjected to interrogation, remember several principles. First, realize that *anyone* can be forced to talk. This is true of spies, military personnel, and businesspeople. You must decide the information you wish to withhold and the information you are willing to share. There is no point in being abused for withholding information that is innocent or is a matter of public record.

If your business organization handles confidential information, the disclosure of which could jeopardize lives, you should have a prearranged plan to deal with this knowledge during interrogation. The plan should include the assumption that classified information *will* be disclosed. Emergency measures must be taken by the business organization to protect those individuals who may be at risk as a result of the disclosure of this information. You can pace your resistance to interrogation to allow the emergency measures to take effect. If you release classified information, do not suffer from guilt.

Resistance to physical abuse during an interrogation is beyond the scope of this book. However, there are tactics that can be used in a non-physical interrogation to either delay or prevent the disclosure of confidential information. Repeated assertions that you do not understand the question, coupled with asking the interrogators to clarify questions, may be helpful. Try to select a piece of the question that you can answer safely and then respond to that portion of the question exhaustively. In other words, be long-winded and talk around the key issue.

## ■ WEAPONS IN CAPTIVITY

You *can* take weapons with you into captivity! While most implements will be removed from your person, your knowledge cannot be taken away. Wisdom or applied knowledge can only be relinquished if it is not used. It can also be lost if you allow yourself to sink into a deep, consuming depression. The weapons everyone takes with them, according to Dr. Rick Farley, former Navy psychologist, are *faith* and *hope*. Whether you are a legitimate military prisoner of war or a prisoner of fate, these weapons cannot be taken away.

Dr. Farley worked with many POWs as well as with the Marine Corps victims of the 444-day Iranian Crisis. He found that the survivors who had faith in God, in their government, or in their organizations were far better equipped to handle personal crises. They also were able to get on with their lives and careers more quickly than those victims who had no faith and hope.

*Trust* is another weapon that can help you. Trust the organization that sent you overseas. If you know that your company will do everything possible to release you, then you will be less likely to slip into a severe depression. Perhaps you can visualize Ross Perot's negotiation and rescue of his employees when they were illegally imprisoned in Teheran.

## ■ COMMUNICATIONS TO THE OUTSIDE

If you are taken hostage, how should you receive a request to write outside communications? In many cases, this is not a problem. Your captors may simply want you to prove you are alive. Some American hostages, particularly those employed by the U.S. Government, have been asked to write confessions, policy denunciations, or humanitarian appeals in their own behalf. Certainly, it is understood by all onlookers that a hostage is not acting as a free agent. Captivity statements can be denied or explained later. You were under extreme duress and you made the statement to protect your own interests.

*During your imprisonment, you should take advantage of any opportunity to communicate to the outside world.* Write letters or speak into tape recorders. Tell the world that you are alive. Because proof-of-life questions must be answered for negotiations to begin, help your captors establish your well-being. The more communication between your captors and the outside world, the sooner you'll be released.

Communicating can also be multidimensional. You may communicate in ways that your captors cannot comprehend.

> This is why having a prearranged signal can be a benefit. Good pre-planning will allow you to give your family signals that can help in finding your location. While in most occasions, these signals are of marginal benefit, at the very minimum they can tell the negotiators of your general condition.[18]

In my studies over the last 2 decades, I have not heard of one businessperson who has been extensively abused during captivity. Even in cases in which the terrorist group wants a businessman to "confess" that he is actually a CIA operative, abuse is not normally on the agenda. Usually, physical duress is not applied to elicit these admissions.

Think of alternative responses to unacceptable statements that would allow you to live. If you make a statement that is taped or video-recorded, or if you write out a message, do it in such a way that your family, friends, and organization will *know* that you are alive and healthy. Indicate that you heard something on the news that day, thereby relating your communication to recent world events. Prove that you are alive on a particular day by what you say or write. This one action will help expedite the entire negotiation process.

If the letter is in *your* handwriting, people who know your writing will be assured that you wrote it. They will also be assured that the note they are reading was not dated earlier. This is a very important indication and can decrease the amount of time you spend in captivity.

## ■ COMMUNICATIONS WITH YOUR CAPTORS

You may really have a problem in talking with your captors. These men and women have a large array of proven psychological techniques to elicit information. Some of these techniques are subtle and many are extremely obvious.

The Red Brigade did not want General James Dozier to hear certain sounds that might later be associated with his "People's Prison." Therefore, they put stereo headphones on his head and increased the volume. He was forced to listen to rock music. A few days later, he was able to negotiate an alternative radio station and was able to listen to light and classical music.

Captain John Testrake of TWA Flight 847 really had a touchy situation. The Shias holding his passengers and plane were not familiar with western toilets. Shia fundamentalists defecate by squatting. Instead of using toilet paper, they clean their rectal area with water. After trudging around in the dust and dirt of the airfield, they would come in, put their feet on the toilet seats, and squat. Then they liberally splashed water all over the restroom facilities, creating a nightmare in terms of cleanliness and hygiene.

Captain Testrake was able to quietly discuss the issue of the different ways the terrorists and their victims used toilet facilities. Without challenging their custom of using the toilet, he was able to negotiate an acceptable situation. Shias and westerners began using separate, designated toilet facilities. The lead Shia actually marked, in Arabic, the designators on the door of the toilets.

## ■ THE HOSTAGE CAN NEGOTIATE TOO

George S. Roukis wrote of terrorist negotiations for the corporate executive. He recommended that the hostage, too, could bargain.

> Roukis emphasizes that the hostage must attempt to cooperate with the captors. This does *not* mean that the captured executive must identify with the terrorists, but he or she must not become competitive. The evidence shows that the cooperative bargaining strategies work best with terrorists, when corporate executives are held hostage. Admittedly, understanding the dynamics of a hostage environment is not enough to allay the emotional distress an executive experiences when kidnapped, but it is possible to train high-risk executives on how to cope with it.[19]

There are some cases where a victim has negotiated his own release. All communications should be conducted from a mind-set that enhances the personal respect and dignity of one individual to the other. Conducting yourself with dignity increases the probability that you will be treated reasonably.

# ■ WOMEN IN CAPTIVITY

Men are ordinarily taken captive by terrorists. Only in a few, rare instances are foreign women taken hostage. Unfortunately, this statement is not also true of the indigenous population where women, as well as children, may be kidnapped as well.

Most mature women are probably more afraid than men in a hostage situation. Men, for the most part, do not have to be concerned with rape or sexual abuse. Privacy issues become much more formidable to the woman taken hostage.

Two women, Catherine Kirby (Colombia—1985) and Eunice Diment (the Philippines—1976), were taken captive by revolutionaries. Catherine Kirby was a rancher in the cattle-raising area of rural Colombia. She was held in a jungle camp for 6 months. Eunice Diment was a linguist working for the Summer Institute of Linguistics in the Philippines. She was held captive for 3 weeks.

Eunice wrote *Kidnapped* about her experiences; Posternoster Press, in England, published the small volume in 1976. Catherine wrote *Terrorist Captive: An Autobiographical Experience*. Both Eunice and Catherine commented on their total loss of privacy. Both of these women, however, did have women guards available at times, but were frequently accompanied and observed by men as they bathed or used the latrines.

Catherine Kirby said that she bathed in streams and rivers with her clothes on. She wore a large, single-piece, native dress that draped out like a tent. When men, instead of women, were watching her, she would remove her undergarments while still in the dress. She would wash her underclothes and then wash her body while standing in 12- to 18-inch-deep water.

Catherine commented on her first "real" bath in their permanent encampment.

> My change of clothes arrived. . . . and I asked to take a bath immediately. This was rather complicated as the bathing spot was in the stream, right in front of the kitchen and general get-together area. They [M-19] bathed in briefs or swimming trunks, the girls with their bras on, and returned to their camp spots to change, sometimes after wrapping a blanket or towel around themselves, or maybe not. The girls wandered around camp with just bra and pants, or perhaps a shirt unbuttoned. All this was quite public and without self-consciousness.
>
> But as for me, a black plastic tarpoleon was strung up on the bank, which gave me some privacy from the kitchen side of the stream, but none at all from the other side. Nanci was my guard and accompanied me to the spot. She assured me that my privacy would be respected. She told me that they were all well-mannered and cultured. I had plenty of doubts, but it was no time for prudery. Modesty and decency, yes, but not prudery.

I decided that I shall always try to insist upon respect and if they respected me, they would have a different idea about all Americans. I admit that my state, physically dirty and smelly after four days of extreme exertion and emotional stress, made me willing to accept almost any condition—however primitive—for a chance to be clean again. I took off all my clothes and submerged myself in the stream with a bar of soap. As far as I know, Nanci was right, for no one bothered me. Afterwards, she helped me to dress, standing on the muddy bank behind the black plastic.[20]

Catherine was 60 years old when she was kidnapped. Whenever a guerilla talked of intimate or sexual things, she would change the subject. She let everyone know that she was not interested in any man except her husband.

Eunice was a much younger woman, however. Her captors assured Sulaiman (her native translator) that she would not be molested and they gave her a similar assurance. For privacy purposes, she wore a large, native tubular skirt. She "used the skirt as a covering when I used the toilet in the bushes."[21] Eunice had a problem because she was unmarried. Eunice could speak many of the local dialects and related well with the village women and children.

There was a lot of teasing from the commanders and the men. They liked the fact that I wore Muslim clothes and could speak their language. It would be very nice, they said, for me to have a Bangingi husband and they suggested that I should marry Commander J. [of the Moro National Liberation Front]. I assured them that I had no intention of marrying anybody there. It occurred to me that perhaps I should try to tone down my image a bit. I didn't want to appear too desirable as a wife. So I abandoned my intention to ask if I could help the women with the food preparation and didn't reveal the fact that I knew how to clean rice. And I stopped taking much interest in the children, since this provoked unwelcome interest too.[22]

Eunice's decision seems to compromise the bonding recommendations made in Chapter 7, but her decisions must be examined in a cultural context. She was bonding so well that they were becoming sexually attracted to her. In the Moslem family, women sleep in separate rooms. Eunice had to claim her cultural privilege to stay with the women on one occasion. She was forced to be assertive, but reasonable, when asked to sleep with one of her abductors. She also veiled her negative response in terms of the culture, in order to make it more acceptable.

# ■ FIGHTING BOREDOM

Boredom is difficult to fight. While some terrorist hostages have enjoyed radio, stereo, television, and even VCR privileges, the majority have not.

Many hostages do not have anything to read—not even a Bible. Others have only communist propaganda available.

Hostages take varying positions or modify their thinking patterns and life-style philosophies to deal with boredom. Dr. Rick Farley, former Navy psychologist, talked about the pilot who played golf in his mind. The pilot replayed every course he had ever visited. While in captivity, he obviously wasn't allowed to play golf, but the score of his first golf game after being released was significantly improved.

U.S. Naval Commander Lloyd Bucher of the *U.S.S. Pueblo* was kept in solitary confinement for 9 of the 12 months spent in captivity.

> One of the mental techniques Bucher used to preserve his sanity was to attempt solving complex mathematical problems mentally. The attempt consumed large amounts of time, as did memory exercizes he devised for himself, such as trying to recall every person Bucher had ever met in his life, starting with his earliest memories. According to Commander Bucher, both of these techniques proved invaluable in saving his sanity during captivity, the length of which he had no way of knowing.[23]

## ■ ATTITUDE DURING CAPTIVITY

While it is difficult to maintain a positive mental attitude during captivity, you must do it. Think and project an attitude of self-respect. Self-aggrandizement or cockiness is not what I mean. *Smart alecks are punished.*

British Ambassador Geoffrey Jackson had the attitude that he was "Her Majesty's Representative," whether in the splendor of a London Palace or the squalor of a Uruguayan prison. He suffered through dysentery and squatted over a water pail while young Tupamaro girls mocked him. But even in this situation, Sir Jackson comported himself admirably.

Bruce Olson, who spent 285 days in ELN captivity during 1988 and 1989 heard the shots and saw the bodies resulting from several revolutionary executions. He was once put in a mock execution himself and thought he was going to be killed. Some members of the firing squad liked him and were actually crying as he was placed before them. They, too, thought he was going to be killed. The guns were empty, however, so all he heard were trigger clicks. He still lives with the memory of that emotional abuse, however.

Anthony Scotti states that there are other problems associated with captivity. Whether you are alone or with a group, you are still surrounded by a hostile environment.

> Besides the smell of unwashed, perspiring bodies and human waste, there will be a sickly odor of fear. There is no place to hide from the nightmare,

no place for tranquility and privacy. The victim has to make his or her tranquility.[24]

Earnest Brace, a civilian American pilot, was shot down over Laos and held for several years by the Viet Cong. In his search for healing, he reviewed the text *Man's Search for Meaning.*

In this book, Victor Frankl [the writer] tells of his captivity in Nazi Germany and of man's ability to overcome evil and control his own destiny. He writes that under such conditions "everything can be taken from a man but one thing; the last of human freedoms—to choose one's attitude in any given set of circumstances, to choose one's own way."[25]

Your attitude is very important. Have faith. Have faith in God, in your family, and in your organization. Keep your faith and your hope as they are necessary survival tools.

## ■ REFERENCES

1. Anthony J. Scotti, *Executive Safety & International Terrorism: A Guide For Travelers* (Englewood Cliffs, NJ: Prentice-Hall Inc., 1986), 175.
2. Terrell E. Arnold and Moorehead Kennedy, *Terrorism: The New Warfare* (New York: Walker and Company, 1988), 92.
3. Scotti, 177.
4. David P. Jacobsen, "My Life As a Hostage," (Los Angeles: *Los Angeles Times Magazine*, March 1, 1987) 3: #9(12).
5. Ibid., 13.
6. Ibid., 14.
7. Ibid., 34.
8. Benjamin and Carol Weir, *Hostage Bound—Hostage Free* (Philadelphia: Westminster Press, 1987), 27.
9. Ibid., 35.
10. Diego and Nancy Asencio, *Our Man Is Inside* (New York: Atlantic-Little, Brown Books, 1983), 7–8.
11. Ibid., 31.
12. Claude Fly, *No Hope But God* (New York: Hawthorn Books, 1973), 31.
13. Fausto Buchelli with J. Robin Maxson, *Hostage!* (Grand Rapids, MI: Zondervan Publishing House, 1982), 232.
14. Ibid., 131.
15. Dan McKinnon, *Everything You Need To Know Before You Are Hijacked* (San Diego, CA: House of Hits Publishers, 1986), 117.
16. Geoffrey Jackson, *The People's Prison* (London: Faber Press, 1973), 33.
17. Fly, 74–75.
18. Scotti, 177.
19. Patrick J. Montana and George S. Roukis (eds.), *Managing Terrorism: Strategies for the Corporate Executive* (Westport, CT: Quorum Books, 1983), xv.

20. Catherine W. Kirby, *Terrorist Captive: An Autobiographical Experience* (Unpublished, 1988), 26.
21. Eunice Diment, *Kidnapped!* (London: The Paternoster Press, 1976), 5.
22. Ibid., 22.
23. Scotti, 176.
24. Ibid., 184.
25. Earnest C. Brace, *A Code to Keep* (New York: Saint Martins Press, 1988), 1.

# 9

## ■■ HOSTAGE NEGOTIATION

An extortion crisis cripples corporations and organizations by throwing up unfamiliar problems that require urgent solutions. Negotiations for a human life are very dynamic and these events place stress on everyone concerned.

Families grieve as though a death has occurred. Organizations react or overreact, depending on whether plans existed before the crisis. The negotiator is caught in the middle. He is a central figure, usually a consultant, and is a part of—yet apart from—the organization and the family.

There are only three alternatives in a hostage situation: attrition, rescue, or negotiation. In attrition, the terrorists or criminals get tired of holding the hostage—his presence is no longer an advantage and they just let him go. Attrition occurs in only a small number of cases. Rescue attempts require force and impose an extreme danger to the hostage. The last alternative, negotiation, is the preferred response in most hostage cases. Negotiation affords time for both sides to consider alternatives that each party can accept without loss of face.

Most business organizations do not have policies that relate to terrorism or extortion-based crises. Many executives and the organizations they run fail to address the issues relating to terrorism. Even after all the hostage incidents taking place all over the world, people do not believe that their business organization could be affected. However, a policy to deal with a hostage crisis is absolutely essential.

## ■ NEGOTIATION POLICIES

[In a hostage situation], we face two dilemmas. The first dilemma is negotiation. *It is the dilemma of courage versus compassion.* That is the one that troubles me the most in my research. I found that *every democratic country, including ours, says publicly that one must not negotiate with terrorists, but in fact every country does.*[1]

U.S. policy has changed over the last several years. It was once said that the U.S. would not negotiate, capitulate, pay ransom, or accede to any extortion demand. Later, our government stated that it talked to terrorists for humanitarian reasons, but would not officially recognize terrorist organizations as legal entities nor would they concede to extortion demands.

> In defense of this [no negotiation] policy, [former Secretary of State] Henry Kissinger noted that the problem of hostage negotiation, at least from the perspective of the government, must be viewed in the context of thousands of Americans who are in jeopardy all over the world. From this perspective, acquiescence to terrorist demands is seen as a stimulus to increased and continuing terror against Americans across the globe.[2]

A pamphlet entitled *International Terrorism: U.S. Policy on Taking American Hostages* was released by the U.S. State Department in June 1986. The following statement summarizes that release:

> The U.S. Government will make no concessions to terrorists holding official or private U.S. citizens hostage. It will not pay ransom, release prisoners, change its policies, or agree to other acts that might encourage additional terrorism. At the same time, the U.S. will use every available resource to gain the safe return of American citizens who are held hostages by terrorists.

However, the U.S. Government has not always followed its own policy. In fact, there are many indications that the policy was violated even as far back as the days of Mediterranean piracy. The Barbary Coast pirates made millions extorting monies for ransoms from individual American citizens.

Even when Clinton Knox, Ambassador to Haiti, was abducted in 1973, there was a ransom payment. The suggestion that Haitian President Francois Duvalier paid the ransom seems rather superficial when millions of dollars in U.S. aid were being channeled into his banks at the time.

Terrorism scholar, Dr. Ariel Merari, suggests that our present policy is ludicrous.

> Quite often, what is intended as toughness against the terrorists actually turns out to be toughness against the victims. *Such a response requires nothing but rhetorical courage.* Rigid sanctions that have not been very successful against ordinary crime will not work at all against crusading terrorism; [these policies] just create a false sense of security.[3]

In talking about the policies of governments, Dr. Merari recommends the "coordinated flexible response pattern." These mixed responses include, but are not limited to, delay, negotiation, promises, firmness, consistency, and force. We should not be chained to any preconceived political or other bias in producing the best results.

Dr. Frederick Hacker, in *Crusaders, Criminals, and Crazies*, said, "I do not advocate softness [nor does this author]. To yield under any circumstance is just as unprofitable and futile as to decide in advance never to yield."[4]

# ■ SHOULD YOU COOPERATE WITH THE HOST GOVERNMENT?

Another major decision for the family and the business organization to make is whether or not to cooperate with the host government. Most westerners are raised to believe in and trust police and military authorities, but while many of the senior officers of police units in developing nations have excellent training, we can not assume that they are equipped to effectively deal with this crisis. Sometimes the police or military authorities may have purposes that are at variance with the goals of the family or business. The police or military may have a priority to kill all terrorists. If they do, your hostage is at real disadvantage if a raid is attempted.

The government may also prioritize terrorist arrests. In this case, capturing a terrorist may take precedence over rescuing or protecting your family member or colleague. Another risk in cooperating with the government is that the government may prevent negotiations entirely or may mandate that monetary payments will not be made. The government often electronically bug the telephone and radio systems available to the business and the hostage's family. This interference may create many problems and an intrusion could even cause a death.

> From the government's point of view, accommodating terrorist demands by paying ransom or extortion and publishing manifestoes only provides the terrorists with the means to continue their attack.[5]

# ■ THE NEGOTIATOR

What does a negotiator actually accomplish in a hostage situation? What should the negotiator do? What should he not do? Certainly it is appropriate to reach some level of understanding about his role. His first priority should be the life of the victim. Every effort to effectively expedite and coordinate the victim's release should be accorded.

The first predicament for the negotiator is to overcome the family's and business organization's erroneous beliefs about crime or terror. He must help them understand that time is an ally, not an enemy.

The family and the representative organization will often put inordinate pressure on the negotiator to solve the problem *"now."* But the negotiator knows that it is usually to the hostage's advantage to lengthen the time of captivity, at least during the early stages of negotiation. There are usually only three exceptions to this rule. The first exception is when a chronic or life-threatening illness impacts the negotiation process.

The second exception occurs if the victim is a temperamental individual. The negotiator will be extraordinarily concerned about the victim's safety if it is believed that the victim will exacerbate the problems of his captivity by temperamental outbursts and continuing conflict. If the victim is rude, arrogant, or disruptive, his life will be in danger. The hostage must control his own behavior and be reasonably polite and courteous. If he is not amenable to common courtesy, the likelihood of death or mistreatment is increased under the get-rid-of-the-jerk approach to hostages in captivity.

The third exception to the time element occurs when reliable information is received that the hostage is being physically mistreated. Physical mistreatment rarely occurs, however, in spite of media hype to the contrary.

Trying to hurry a hostage resolution will probably have a negative impact on all aspects of the negotiation and may even considerably increase the amount of time a hostage remains in captivity. Most experts agree that time is always to the advantage of the hostage. One well-known expert, however, disagrees.

H.H.A. Cooper, President of Nuevevidas (Nine Lives) International is the only vocal critic of this concept of whom I am aware. An experienced negotiator and an excellent writer, Cooper gives a very reasonable opposing viewpoint.

> [Time] is a commodity, like any other, which can be wasted or put to good use. The hostage negotiator must not let false notions about time affect his thinking or his tactics. *Every contemplated action should be adapted to the time available for its accomplishment.*[6]

Statistical reviews indicate that 98% of all hostages leave captivity safely after a negotiated settlement, but only 86% leave after a rescue attempt. Some 79% of all hostage deaths occur during rescue attempts.[7] This factor gives administrators a lot to consider. A high percentage of rescued hostages are shot or killed by the rescue unit, not by the adversaries.

> The record [nevertheless] indicates that the longer a hostage and barricade episode lasts, the more often hostages come out alive—and episodes have been getting longer as governments increasingly refuse to meet terrorist demands.[8]

## ■ PICK A TRAINED AND EXPERIENCED NEGOTIATOR

One of the most difficult decisions a family or a business organization must face is picking a professional negotiator. Second-quality services and third-rate information can cause grave injury and even death. If your intention is to attempt a rescue, then you will need to select a soldier trained in counter-terrorism or a policeman experienced in Special Weapons Assault Team (SWAT) methods. However, if you want to negotiate an expedited release, you should employ the services of an experienced negotiator. The hostage negotiator must be chosen based on his attributes. He must be cool, resourceful, mature, and, above all, effective in verbal communication.

In the United States, most hostage negotiators are experienced police officers or detectives who have a gift for talking with criminals and social deviants. Psychiatrists were used for a year or two as negotiators, but were later replaced. Their counseling-treatment mode of dealing with terrorists was often unacceptable.

The negotiator should be assertive. It was quickly determined that police officers and detectives who deal with criminals, the mentally disturbed, and revolutionaries on a daily basis were more assertive and more successful in negotiating a successful hostage release. The psychiatrists were not sufficiently direct. Health-related professionals are still consulted and are often called to the scene of a barricade/hostage encounter, but police officers negotiate, not psychologists or psychiatrists.

Robert Kupperman, renown terrorism consultant and author, says that the primary qualities of a negotiator include

1. volunteers only,
2. who are in excellent physical and emotional condition.
3. They should be psychologically sound and
4. have a mature appearance.
5. They should also be outgoing and
6. have a good speaking voice . . . Above all, they must be good communicators.[9]

H.H.A. Cooper has some additional advice. His suggestions should be carefully considered as he is one of the most experienced professionals in the field of international hostage negotiation.

> The hostage negotiator must be a person capable of working effectively under intense pressure. He must care for others, but not to the point where his objectivity is impaired. He will need considerable personal courage, not only of the kind that will sustain him in situations of immediate physical danger, but of the type that will enable him to operate with equanimity in the face of adversity and criticism. Patience is an indispensable virtue, the kind that informs action and allows it to take place at its proper time. The good negotiator is a moderate in all things, being neither a zealot nor a sluggard, but he should not be "wishy-washy." He should be capable of taking a position and arguing strenuously for it, but he should be receptive to counter arguments without tending toward vacillation. His firmness must not be the product of blinkered vision. He should be tough but flexible, knowing when to bend without breaking.[10]

If your organization is working in a high-risk environment, it may be wise to go negotiator shopping *before* an incident occurs. You will need to find someone in whom you have confidence and who understands your business organization. Within reason, he must be willing to follow corporate policies. If he cannot or will not, then he will most likely refuse the contract, stating his reasons for doing so.

When searching for a negotiator, you should be just as thorough as you would be during an executive candidate examination or when serving on a Chief Executive Officer (CEO) search committee. Some personnel specialists use the acronym *KSAPC* when searching for any job candidate— Knowledge, Skill, Ability, and Personal Characteristics. Certainly this standard is necessary when searching for a hostage negotiator. The following questions should be asked of a potential negotiator and should help you establish a base from which to select a negotiator:

1. State your general experiences in the area of hostage negotiation.
2. Have you ever successfully negotiated the release of a captive businessperson, government employee, humanitarian agency representative, or missionary?
3. Give case examples and files on newspaper accounts. Insist that the potential negotiater *prove* his claims.
4. Have you ever paid a ransom? If so, how much? What was the first dollar amount demanded in this incident?
5. What is your fee?
6. How are your expenses computed?

You should then check all of the statements and all of the references. Do not expect to see the negotiator's name in newspaper accounts or media releases that reference the incident. Professional hostage negotiators maintain a very low profile.

You should also talk with the members of a family or business organization of a former hostage. Would they recommend your potential negotiator? You should also ask the negotiator,

1. Did you leave behind hurt feelings, angry government officials, or other problems for the organization to clean up?
2. Did you violate any of the host country's laws in dealing with the terrorists? If yes, were these acts absolutely necessary to save the hostage's life?
3. Were you discreet? Or did you cause later problems for the family or the organization?

You also need to discover the full facts about any negotiations made by your potential negotiator. If the first ransom demand was for $500,000 in U.S. currency and the negotiator paid $250,000, then he really did not help the family or sponsoring organization that much. The percentage of terroristic extortion actually paid is usually between 10% and 25% of the original demand.

In several instances, organizations have been able to obtain a release without paying any ransom whatsoever. They did not bow to extortion demands in any way. Sometimes a negotiated settlement can be obtained for *direct expenses*. Direct expenses normally include the actual accumulated indebtedness and normal daily wage of the hostage-takers. Meals, blankets, essentials, gasoline, and other automobile expenses are also normally computed into the expense factor, as well. But the final release payment may be $5,000 in U.S. currency or even less, instead of the $250,000–$500,000 original ransom demand.

If your negotiator has not served in the region or country where your hostage is being held, he will need cultural conditioning and should begin a self-training program using local maps, an atlas, geographical surveys, and books about the country and its culture. He should also study intelligence data in relation to the group holding or believed to be holding your hostage. It is helpful if your negotiator is already fully knowledgeable about the culture, the language, and the terrorist group holding the hostage, but this is not always necessary. While all of these qualities are ideal, it is much more important that your negotiator understand terrorism, the terrorists as individuals, and the negotiation process.

The negotiator selection process is very important. If hostage negotiation is your potential negotiator's only method of earning a living, then his professional pride about his reputation may intrude and his ego may become antithetical to the settlement process. Carefully analyze all the statements he makes as you interview your potential negotiator prior to appointment.

## ■ STAY WITH YOUR NEGOTIATOR

If the hostage negotiator is doing a good job, the terrorists may ask that he be discharged. They may want to negotiate with a local business representative or attorney. This will be a difficult decision for the Crisis Management Team (CMT). Should you acquiesce or should you stand firm? In most cases, you should stand firm. The only exception occurs when the CMT evaluates the negotiator as being incompetent or as having an excessive attraction toward alcohol or drugs. These tendencies will actually affect the quality of the negotiation process. However, if you asked the *right* questions during the pre-employment interviews, this type of evaluation is not likely to occur.

Ask yourself, Would you fire your lawyer during the middle of a lawsuit? If so, under what circumstances? What reasons would be appropriate for dismissal? If the lawyer is doing a good job, do not let him go. The same is true in a hostage situation. If the terrorists are negotiating with a competent professional instead of a frightened family member or an uninformed businessperson, then most likely they would want the negotiator fired. They want to negotiate with an unprepared and uninformed negotiator, not with a professional.

While the process will be frightening, the CMT should insist that only their negotiator will speak for them and that a proof-of-life question will be asked before each session. Forcing the proof-of-life question during the negotiation increases the victim's chances and makes it easier to obtain concessions later during the negotiation process.

## ■ WHERE DO CORPORATIONS GET THEIR NEGOTIATORS?

The Rand Corporation has written extensively on the subject of terrorism. Susanna W. Purnell and Eleanor S. Wainstein wrote *The Problems of U.S. Businesses Operating Abroad in Terrorist Environments*. This Rand document is one of the best contributions to this field. The researchers interviewed many corporate leaders and sent questionnaires to others. Under the topic of selecting hostage negotiators, those queried had the following to say about their work with U.S. corporations abroad:

> Respondents indicated that corporate officials select negotiators from among a variety of sources, including the home, country, and regional offices; security consultant firms; and other outsiders. Several respondents advised against assigning someone from the local operation, because of his possible personal involvement with the hostage.
>
> In over half of the cases we examined, the corporation used a national of the country in which the kidnapping occurred as its contact with the terrorists, so as to avoid misunderstandings due to language or cultural differences. One firm, for example, employed a local lawyer who had acted successfully as the point of contact in a previous kidnapping. In fact, of our 15 respondents involved in negotiations, only two ever talked with the terrorists and one of the two was a foreign national.[11]

Local business representatives can help the negotiator acquire cultural sensitivity and the official translator can ensure that appropriate interpretations occur to enhance the communication process. In fact, the interpretation process may enhance the quality of communication, because the process itself gives the principle negotiator extra time to consider statements as the interpreter translates conversations.

The terrorist translator should be heard by the hostage negotiator and the terrorist's negotiator. This is true even if the western negotiator is using

English. While languages cannot always be translated perfectly, the voice, even over a telephone, can communicate moods and feelings in many other ways. If negotiations occur over the phone, the negotiator can immediately begin bargaining, and making and obtaining concessions. The first concession requested should be a proof-of-life question and answer. The second concession obtained should be a requirement that the hostage be allowed to write a personal letter to a family member.

## ■ SHOULD A LOCAL BUSINESS REPRESENTATIVE NEGOTIATE?

Normally, the practice of allowing a local business representative to negotiate is unacceptable.

Death threats are usual in these events and they are very intimidating and frightening. A death threat against your colleague may decrease your objectivity and you may not be able to carry through as a competent negotiator. If the event goes awry, the negotiator will feel terribly guilty. If the hostage dies or is killed while trying to escape, the friend who negotiates is much more likely to be damaged emotionally than the trained negotiator. The friend will later ask himself a thousand questions while analyzing the events as they happened. What if I had done this differently? What if? The "what ifs" can debilitate the effectiveness of the entire organization, not to mention that of the negotiator. This situation should not be allowed. The organization can keep this from happening by bringing in an outside, experienced hostage negotiator.

## ■ FACILITATORS

In several hostage events, the terrorist group holding the hostage communicated through a local politician, church official (often associated with the Left), or local attorney. They did not speak with any other person. These groups may refuse to speak with anyone that they do not know personally. Perhaps they trust a local pastor or priest. Using locals can also be a problem because the terrorist group can also intimidate him and threaten his family with statements like "We know where to find you."

Under *no* circumstances should the business organization or family member allow the facilitator to take a leadership role. Remember that you need this person. He is the information conduit first established by the terrorists and may be the only source that is ever revealed during the negotiations. Again, you *need* this person to obtain information, to intervene on behalf of the victim, and to transmit information. It is very important, however, to ensure that this person serves *only* as a communicator. He should not and, under most circumstances, must not become part of the CMT or the decision-making process. He should not even be present when decisions are made, although he should be allowed to communicate to the CMT when it is in session.

The facilitator, like the locally assigned business manager, is too close to the problem and too close to the people. If he lives in the area where your hostage is held, he may be threatened and intimidated. He may slip up or reveal some aspect of your negotiation strategy. He cannot be given the information to do this. In this way, no one in his family can discuss or even gossip about the crisis because they do not know what is happening.

> Every effort should be made to establish a real bond between the hostage negotiator and these third parties, and they should be encouraged to see themselves as working with the authorities toward a common goal. In many of these cases, the parties will relate better on a personal basis than they would to an institution or organization which they might tend to view in adversarial terms. The hostage negotiator should never be patronizing to these persons. . . . If it is worth seeking their collaboration to try to bring matters to a satisfactory conclusion, they should be accorded the proper respect for their endeavors. They may be frightened, embarrassed, angry, or even hostile, but it is up to the negotiator to put them at ease so they can function effectively. . . . it is clear that the negotiator can make a vital difference.[12]

Communicating information back and forth between terrorists and the hostage negotiator is not negotiating—it is reporting. The facilitator must submit to the authority of the organization's CMT and to the instructions of the negotiator. If the facilitator decides that he is in charge, if he takes actions not previously approved by the CMT, or if he takes off on his own initiative, he may cause incalculable harm. You simply cannot let him do this.

In some cases, there may be a gnawing concern that the facilitator is working in concert with the revolutionaries, rather than for the hostage. Why was *he* selected by the revolutionaries? Why was someone else in his community not selected? If the person first approached by the terrorists is not well-known in the local community, be cautious. Surely you want to obtain all the information available, but you need *good* and *reliable* information from a creditable source, not questionable information.

The CMT from your organization must remain in charge. Even the negotiator is normally a consultant to the CMT and cannot vote on issues, though he can (and should) influence the decisions through his recommendations. Certainly a CMT would be poorly advised to go against his expert advice.

# ■ THE TRANSLATOR

A good translator is also important in the negotiation process. The negotiator must ensure that an appropriate interpretation occurs and this is quite often difficult to accomplish. Some bilingual negotiators still use interpreters even though they understand the language perfectly well. Even as the translation occurs, they are able to think longer about their answers for they hear the message twice. The bilingual negotiator can also double-check primary meanings in two languages to ensure the best communication.

The best translator available should be used, but he should also be trusted for his discretion. Sometimes cultural advice as well as linguistic counsel is obtained. This ensures that the words and the tone are correct and acceptable. The negotiator must ensure that his opposing communicant understands what he is saying and understands his position. The terrorist needs to be able to follow the logic of the negotiator's reasoning.

As in the case of the facilitator, you must ensure that the translator does not attempt to take over the negotiation process. If the translator has a superficial understanding of the negotiation philosophy, he can really intrude on the process. This must not happen. The negotiator must be in charge of the discussion and the translator must be loyal to the negotiator.

# ■ THE NEGOTIATOR'S OFFICE

The CMT should normally establish operations away from the victim's home or office. These locations are too public and there are too many probable disrupters. Move the operation to another office. Crisis management discussions should be held privately and away from potential eavesdroppers. Casual discussions or gossip about CMT work can get a hostage killed. If a CMT has a "leak," the source should be determined quickly. In some instances the source should be dismissed.

The negotiator will also need certain equipment. He will tape record all negotiations, if possible. He needs general office equipment and a word processor. He will need the equipment necessary to monitor the news, including radio, television, and the print media, for all references to the incident. A portable shortwave receiver is a great advantage in countries that allow their importation. Sometimes, news reports from other areas of the world are more substantial and detailed than local news accounts. The shortwave tuned in to the British Broadcasting Commission (BBC), The Voice of America, or the U.S. Armed Forces Radio and Television Network, may be a real advantage.

In many instances, the media cannot be trusted. The level of responsible journalism is much lower in many of the developing nations. In any country, including the United States, you may read a lot of propaganda or statements that are self-serving to particular agencies, governments, or administrative policies. The truth may be overstated, understated, or distorted. But in countries where ethics do not always exist in journalism, you may read fiction and lies, which are being represented as the truth.

## ■ WHAT ARE YOU NEGOTIATING FOR?

In most cases, you are negotiating for freedom for your hostage, but in some instances you must negotiate for the life of your hostage. On occasion, a business organization may be instructed to leave a particular region entirely to secure the hostage's release. In other situations, the extortion demands concern money, land, automobiles, trucks, and airplanes.

Even though the terrorist or criminal predictably acts in his own best interest, he still will be seeking to enter a meaningful dialogue—this is the strength of the negotiator's position. The negotiator does have something that his opponent wants. The negotiator has power and influence over money, property, and publicity. This is where the negotiator first gains the advantage. *The situation is not hopeless—in fact, it is filled with hope!*

## ■ TRUTH-TELLING

The negotiator must have a reputation for credibility. If the negotiator is caught in a lie or a blatant misrepresentation, then his utility in all future negotiations is limited. On the other hand, a distortion of fact made by the hostage-holders can be capitalized on as the negotiator seeks concessions.

This is another reason that local business representatives should not negotiate for the life of a loved one or colleague. Sometimes a degree of deception is necessary in order to buy time or create effective tensions that may aid in resolving the process. The time purchased through a delaying tactic may be extremely critical. In fact, it could save the captive's life.

When administrators and high-level managers are not present, the use of deception is not normally necessary. Assume that a group has answered your proof-of-life question. You now know that the faction you are dealing with has *your* hostage. You know that the hostage was alive and in sufficient health to answer the proof-of-life question. The terrorists now give you 24 hours to raise $20,000 and they threaten to execute the hostage if you do not comply with their deadline.

The terrorists can probably give you a list of all the business representatives present in the country at any given time. They can probably also tell you (to the penny) how much money you have in each and every business and personal bank account in their country, perhaps even on the continent.

Therefore, *a hostage negotiator is not advised to lie, under any circumstances.*

Neither is he advised or compelled to tell the complete and absolute truth. A full disclosure of all facts will disrupt the negotiation process. It will be like playing cards in a room full of mirrors. Your fellow players will always know the cards you can play. A simple business negotiation is like purchasing a car. If you are trying to get a good deal, you might say that you cannot afford the asking price, even though you have that amount in your checking account. By negotiating, your position may improve.

By using the tactic of saying, "the business cannot pay ransom, but the family is desperately trying to raise money for the release," you are not saying "no" and you are not saying "never" to their ransom demands. You are simply indicating to the terrorists their unreasonable expectations of receiving large sums of money. *You are lowering the bounty.*

The negotiator must first discover the stated objectives for the abduction. He then must discover the "real" agenda, because what the terrorists say and what they want are often different. The negotiator must somehow discern the truth in order to form his negotiation strategy. He must use good information, strong intelligence, and must make objective evaluations of all incoming information.

The negotiator must evaluate and reevaluate all information from the hostage-takers. Certainly, he cannot trust them; they will tell any lie to increase pressure on the family or the corporation. They will speak of imminent death or execution, or state that poor health is threatening the life of the hostage. In some instances, the terrorist will extract hostile letters from the hostage. "Why haven't you negotiated my release? If you really cared, I would already be free. These people are reasonable, please work with them for my release." These letters are designed to make family members and organizational executives feel guilty.

The terrorists believe that they have all the power, because they have the hostage. They do not have the power, however. In fact, if they had real power, they would not have taken your business representative as a captive. The terrorists probably feel very vulnerable; perhaps they are frightened or paranoid.

The terrorists may say, "the hostage has malaria and is seriously ill. We are afraid that he will die. You need to settle this matter quickly." The negotiator has an advantage now. The terrorists are probably not telling the truth, but if the victim does have a history of malaria or any other disorder, you can throw their words back onto the bargaining table. "The family and the business are negotiating for a healthy man. If you can not assure me of his health, then these negotiations are invalidated. Take him to a hospital." For the record, many captives have been examined or treated by physicians while they were in captivity.

The negotiator can easily say, "I am negotiating for the life of a well man." The statement would be totally incongruent from a business friend who happened to be pressed into the negotiation process. The negotiator can reasonably say, "I am just a consultant, I never met the hostage. Certainly, I do not want him to die, but if he does, it seems to me that it is your problem and not mine. If you guys have mistreated him, he will probably die after he is released anyway. I have to look at this issue as a professional. If he dies, you folks will be the losers. I will just get on a plane and go to my next assignment."

The suffering of the victim is the leverage used in negotiation. Suffering is certainly an important consideration to a family or corporation, although the suffering may not really exist; the terrorists may feign the matter. The negotiator, who deals with human suffering all the time, cannot let the *threat* of suffering influence his professional decisions. In most cases, the threats are just threats. In cases where it is obvious the hostage is really in bad health, the CMT may dictate an entirely different tactic for the negotiator. This move is acceptable, for *they* are in charge, not the negotiator.

## ■ WHEN NEGOTIATION BEGINS

In some cases, there is a clear and obvious linkage to a hostage-taking incident—a particular group has taken your hostage. In other cases, however, there may not be a clear or visible association. In Colombia today, there are more than 100 groups, subgroups, and splinter groups using terror tactics. Hostage-takers may belong to more than one terror group or be known to cooperate with others. Sometimes, terrorists or former terrorists just kidnap as any other criminal would. They need some money and decide to extort it from kidnapping. Terrorists do not always take formal or visible responsibility for their actions. Sometimes weeks or even months go by before acknowledgments are made or negotiations are initiated.

When the group holding a hostage takes no action to contact the family or the business, a real dilemma occurs. An assortment of extortionists, con artists, and frauds will now try to extract monies from the family or business organization. This is why a proof-of-life question is absolutely essential. Sometimes 10 to 15 individuals or groups will claim possession of the captive. You will never know which one, if any, is telling the truth unless you ask proof-of-life questions and insist that negotiations only begin when you hear the correct answers.

This stance does not mean that you will not listen to whomever or whatever group calls. It simply means that negotiations do not start until the proof-of-life questions are correctly answered. Obviously, this ensures that the group claiming to hold your hostage actually has him. It indicates that the hostage was alive at the time he was asked the question. A simple question will suffice for a proof-of-life question, such as, "What was the name of the dog the hostage had throughout high school?"

The negotiator should also indicate that he will not continue discussions until another proof-of-life question has been answered. This process has three attributes. The first is that it affirms that the hostage is still alive and is in sufficient health to answer the question. The second is that the victim will become aware that release efforts are being made in his behalf. The third attribute is that you refuse to negotiate until the questions are answered. Compliance with this coerced action increases the probability that you can extract future demands, as well. It gets the terrorists used to doing what the negotiator tells them to do. It is the most effective and sometimes the only power play the negotiator has at his immediate disposal.

In deciding to negotiate, one needs the answers to four questions:

1. Who are the hostage-takers?
2. What do they want?
3. What are they prepared to accept?
4. What are we prepared to offer?

The business organization has often been told not to compromise, not to negotiate, not to make deals, and certainly not to pay a ransom. Businesses were instructed in this manner by our government *even when U.S. agencies and many U.S. businesses were not following these guidelines.*

Certainly there are things for which we can legitimately negotiate, under any circumstances. If an area is too dangerous, you could leave for a few weeks or even a few months. There are other alternatives, as well, regarding a ransom payment.

A business should never pay cash, as it could be traded for guns, ammunition, explosives, or even drugs. The business, however, might be willing to build a clinic, donate medicines to help a tribe fight disease, feed a starving population, give blankets to the poor, or help support some other physical or humanitarian need. An organization that would not consider a $10,000 ransom might be willing to give $50,000 in food and medical supplies or spend even more on an acceptable substitute.

If you do not negotiate, you will never even know your options. In fact, the kidnapping could turn into a vital service or a money-making opportunity. But if you have closed your mind by always saying "no" or "never" to extortion demands, you will never know what opportunities you've missed.

Since both sides want the hostage freed, there is a lot of room for what many managers call *win-win negotiations.* Both sides can get something out of the crisis. Most important, however, is the life of the hostage. "The negotiator is seeking to establish dialogue, not argument; he seeks agreement, not divergence."[13]

The captors have a hostage and say that they are willing to execute him. This is certainly a dangerous situation but we do not have to negotiate from a position of weakness. After all, they want something from you, even if it is really only publicity. In many incidents the media attention itself, is the one and only goal.

## ■ CAN FAMILIES INTRUDE UPON THE NEGOTIATION PROCESS?

Families *can* intrude upon the negotiation process. Here is what one hostage negotiator said about his experiences with families:

> Families can impede the recovery operation in a number of ways. They can, [intrude] through advertisements or press leaks, attempt to open their own communication with the terrorists, conveying an attitude that may well be at variance with the negotiating posture selected by the crisis managers. Or they can open a legal or press offensive against the corporation, diverting the energies of crisis managers and possibly causing them to deviate from a valid game plan.[14]

Families should be frequently consulted and their emotional and physical needs should be considered. Families also have special financial problems during the crisis and sensitive organizations should carefully consider their problems and needs. One hostage negotiator explains the family perspective in this way:

> In case after case, families have run the risk of riding the emotional roller coaster as they await the fate of a loved one. There are no easy answers, but it seems that family members must achieve a balance and believe that the victim will be released. Sure, slow moving negotiations or a bad turn in foreign affairs may bring anxiety and depression. *But never lose hope.* Believe in tomorrow—your loved one does.[15]

By working *with* the family, the organization can avoid most problems. If the family understands the problems and the probable solutions, enmity does not develop.

## ■ THE SAFE RELEASE

The time of release is a very difficult time, as well. In some cases, the extortion demand is paid, yet the hostage is not released for an extended period of time. In Italy, at the height of a kidnapping epidemic, some kidnappers would double-cross the family and insist upon more money, even after they had accepted the final offer in good faith. Fortunately, this does not happen often. In some very few cases, the hostage is killed in spite of a ransom being paid.

Increasingly, even when the hostage is ultimately released, the abductors hold on to the captive for an additional 2 to 4 weeks after the ransom is paid. The kidnappers seek assurance that the money is not marked or counterfeit and they ensure that no electronic tracking or eavesdropping equipment was placed with the money.

> After Exxon Oil paid the 14.2 million dollar ransom for Victor Samuelson in Argentina, the kidnappers took *six weeks* to launder the money, bringing Samuelsons' total captivity to five months.[16]

This period of waiting, after the negotiations are concluded and the ransom is paid, is devastating. Perhaps this is the worst of all the stresses endured during the negotiation. Will the abductors keep their word? Will they let the hostage live? Has the hostage been abused? Has the hostage been emotionally impaired by this incident?

At this time, the family and the organization must trust in a higher power. There is nothing else that will help them now; nothing else will give them peace. Mankind has nothing but platitudes to offer or statistical analyses relating to probability. Only a spiritual value system and faith in God can help at this time.

## ■ REFERENCES

1. John G. Stoessinger, "Facing Today's Dilemmas," *Security Management* (Washington, DC: The American Society for Industrial Security, 31 (12) (December 1987), 76.
2. Abraham H. Miller, *Terrorism and Hostage Negotiation* (Boulder, CO: Terrorism, Westview Press, 1980), 19.
3. Ariel Merari, "Government Policy in Incidents Involving Hostages," *On Terrorism and Combatting Terrorism* (New York: University Publications of America, 1985), 165.
4. Frederick Hacker, *Crusaders, Criminals, and Crazies* (New York: W.W. Norton, 1976), 338.
5. Patrick J. Montana and George S. Roukis, *Managing Terrorism: Strategies for the Corporate Executive* (Westport, CT: Greenwood Press, 1983), 126.
6. H.H.A. Cooper, "Establishing A Hostage Negotiation Capability: Operational Precepts," (Gaithersburg, MD: The International Association of Chiefs of Police, 1989), 23.
7. Brian Jenkins, Jona Johnson, and David Ronfeldt, *Numbered Lives: Some Statistical Observations from 77 International Episodes* (Santa Monica: Rand Corporation, July 1977), 27.
8. Gail Bass, Brian A. Jerkins, Konrad Kellen, and David Ronfeldt, *Options*

*for U.S. Policy on Terrorism* (Santa Monica: Rand Corporation (R-2764-RC), July 1981), 4.

9. Robert Kupperman and Daniel Trent, *Terrorism: Threat, Reality, and Response* (Stanford: Hoover Institution Press, 1979), 402.

10. H.H.A. Cooper, *Establishing Hostage Negotiation Capability: Conceptual and Pragmatic Groundwork* (Gaithersburg, MD: The International Association of Chiefs of Police, Group and Area Studies, Tactics and Countermeasures, 1989), 10–11.

11. Susanna W. Purnell and Eleanor S. Wainstein, *The Problems of U.S. Businesses Operating Abroad in Terrorist Environments* (Santa Monica: Rand Corporation (R-2842-DOC), November 1981), 40.

12. H.H.A. Cooper, 6.

13. Ibid., 17.

14. E.C. "Mike" Ackerman, "The Hostage Recovery," *Terrorism and Personal Protection* (Boston: Butterworth Publishers, 1985), 300.

15. Stephen Sloan, *The Pocket Guide To Safe Travel* (New York: Contemporary Books, 1986), 58.

16. Susanna W. Purnell and Eleanor S. Wainstein, 45.

# PART IV

CRISIS PLANNING
MANAGEMENT

# 10

## ■■ RISK ASSESSMENTS

Policies and plans should evolve from an analysis of perceived risk. You need to know what you are up against—what you might face—before you begin your planning process. You won't know which policies are necessary until you have assessed your risk factors. A lot of research should be afforded to this process. You can't use a Ouija Board or roll dice to get your numeric variables.

The term *risk assessment* seems a vague and an elusive term and appears difficult to understand. You may say, "I'm a businessperson. I am not in the intelligence service and do not want to be. I prefer to remain in my own job. Let the security department handle this job."

A risk assessment should be accomplished at all dangerous locations. If you do not have a security department or if your security personnel are thousands of miles away, you need to know the rudiments of assessing risk. The word *risk* basically implies any possibility of loss or an attack of some sort. Risk assessments can be understood by anyone trained to do it and willing to conscientiously complete the task. To make a risk assessment, you should collect the information you need from a variety of public and media sources. Evaluate the information you receive and quantify it to a level of statistical significance or demonstrate that the information is not creditable. Risk analyses are usually completed by any formal business organization.

Several businesses have been established to perform risk assessments for international organizations. Business Risks International (BRI) of Arlington, Virginia; Risk Assessment Ltd. of Waldorf, Maryland; and Control Risks Group (CRG) of Bethesda, Maryland, are good examples. The Bank of America and most of the Fortune 500 companies have professionally modeled risk assessment divisions attached to their assets protection division.

These risk assessment organizations and units can give you good information if you develop an ongoing relationship with them. On occasion, a risk analysis department may be able to give a better quality report than you may receive from the U.S. State Department Emergency Service Hotline, The Overseas Security Advisory Council, or some of the news services.

## ■ HAVE YOU BEEN SURPRISED LATELY?

If an organization is surprised at the onset of a crisis, it seems apparent that something was missing in the organization's contingency planning. If whatever is occurring is significantly serious to constitute a crisis, it must be presumed that had the organization known of, or anticipated the event, it would have prepared for it. From this, it logically follows that the organization, for whatever reason, was not aware of the potential for the crisis to occur, at least at a level of awareness that triggered action.[1]

You need to know your enemy. Knowledge is a weapon you can use to protect your own interests and is your first line of defense. Keeping track of incidents, collating events, cutting out news articles on indigenous terrorism and criminal attacks from newspapers and magazines, and making notes from radio and television broadcasts (noting station number, date, and time) may render an invaluable service. You will have reliable accounts from which to make informed decisions. You, your family, and your organization become safer as you learn about what is happening in your area.

The worst place to obtain information is the rumor mill. Patrick Collins, author of *Living In Troubled Lands,* says the rumor mill will *always* provide unsolicited information.[2] Everything you hear that may influence your security should be verified through creditable sources. The material presented in this chapter will help you verify and quantify the quality and credibility of information you obtain. This material will familiarize you with the various sources of information that are available concerning the risks on various continents. These sources can displace the dangerous rumor mills. "Rumors and rumor mills make for good gossip . . . but they have no place whatever in your security planning or information gathering."[3]

## ■ LOOK FOR TRENDS AND PATTERNS

When looking at broad statistical patterns, it is easy to overlook specific data. For instance, you might be stationed in Panama. There may be many incidents of disorder in a given month. Where do these violent incidents occur? Against whom are they targeted? Are you likely to be caught up in the violence? Could you be caught up in it, incidentally, during the course of a normal day? If you are in Colombia or even in Lebanon, your location may be quite secure, but if you must drive or travel through a dangerous area to get to a hospital or an airport in an emergency, then you may not be safe at all.

There may be hundreds of violent incidents in your host country each month. Are these violent encounters ever directed against Americans or western citizens? Incidents of violence may not occur on a statistically significant basis, but even a single terrorist becomes "statistically significant" if he is pointing a gun at you.

# ■ HOW WILL YOUR COMPANY MANAGE RISK?

There are several major decisions to make in the handling of risk. Is the company going to manage your risk? Or is the company going to allow risk to manage it? The company can act by being proactive or it can be constantly reactive. It can let someone else (perhaps a revolutionary) direct its activities in numerous ways.

A senior executive can make the appropriate risk decisions before an attack occurs. Almost any activity or reaction to risk is going to cost money, but you can decide, now, how your resources may be best applied. There are five outcomes that you can weigh:

> You can buy too little security, thereby incurring an unacceptably high risk. You can buy too much security and spend [waste] money unnecessarily. You can buy the wrong kind of security and lose both ways. You can pay too much for too little security; also losing both ways. Or you can reduce your risk of loss in proportion to the security you buy, or in other words, you can get the best return for the dollars spent on security.[4]

G.S. Shackle is credited with one listing of risk management. He enumerated this account in his text *Decision, Order, and Time in Human Affairs*. This method was also recounted in Joe B. Flynn's excellent book *Design of Executive Protection Systems*. Generally, there are five methods of risk reduction:

1. Risk avoidance—attempting to remove the executive from or lower his exposure to locations and periods of risk.
2. Occurrence reduction—attempting to reduce the activities during which the executive will be threatened.
3. Risk acceptance—allowing a risk or threat to exist due to one's inability to deal with it, but with an intensified monitoring of that risk.
4. Risk spreading—assigning functions to multiple individuals so that the corporate impact upon loss is reduced.
5. Risk transference—using insurance programs to transfer the dollar liability for the loss to another party.

Risk specialist and textbook author John M. Carroll says that there are five ways to manage risk, but he describes them differently. The Carroll method includes:

1. Modifying your environment (run away). Get into a less risky business; move to a safer neighborhood; live in a fortress.
2. Reduce your exposure (hide).
3. Modify loss-causing events (fight back).
4. Mitigate the effects of loss (fall back and regroup). Purchase insurance policies; make duplicate copies of all important documents; arrange to operate at an alternate site in case of interruption.
5. Do nothing (stand pat). The loss-causing event may never occur and if it does, the loss we sustain may be less than the cost of trying to defend against it.[5]

# ■ RISK-FORECASTING AND EVALUATION SYSTEMS

There are many forecasting and evaluation systems. Some are very complex. Some are reviewed and amended on a daily basis through the use of supercomputers. These machines use many variables and data formats to analyze risk data. Several of these systems will be mentioned in this chapter. You should develop a simple and reliable system appropriate for use in your organization.

Steven Fink, who wrote *Crisis Management: Planning for the Inevitable,* developed and documented a risk-forecasting and evaluation system in his text, which is now published by the American Management Association. The system is a simple one and is an excellent system for the business environment. Fink's system can be used by anyone who has the scale denominators and the directions on how to use his method.

Fink says that you must quickly identify a crisis, quickly isolate the crisis, and quickly manage the crisis. To do this well, a predictive measurement device is needed. He developed a *Crisis Impact Scale,* a *Crisis-Plotting Grid,* and a *Crisis Barometer* to assist the risk-assessment process. Fink recommends several measurements in his book, some of which are outlined in this chapter.

The men and women who are now a part of the risk analysis profession come from many diverse backgrounds. Political, economic, and criminal trends can be examined, compared, and analyzed. Any trend that may impact the expatriate organization should be examined.

Most of the business vulnerability and assessment units came into being after 1970. Academics, diplomats, former government employees, translators, journalists, and international business professionals were brought into the field to aid the analysts. Their skills were incorporated into the risk analysis systems used. These professionals are also trained in analytical methods. Data systems were developed that could quantify the information. Then quality control tests were completed.

Some of these formats are quite simple. In Bolivia, for instance, there have been nearly 200 coups d'état during the last three decades. You could almost establish a mathematical formula. It might run something like this

$$X + Y = R$$

where X = political or state repression
    Y = the presence of insurgency forces
    R = revolution

But this is almost too simple. While a statistician could probably prove the theorem with precise logic, the formula would not apply to countries where there is political or state repression, but no presence of insurgency forces and no revolution.

## ■ LOSS-EVENT PROBABILITY

Security specialists Richard J. Healy and Timothy J. Walsh developed a *loss-event probability theorem.* They said,

> We know from elementary statistics that the probability is measured as the number of ways in which a particular event can result from certain activity, divided by the number of events which could occur from that activity. This is
>
> $$P = f/N$$
>
> where   P = the probability that a given event will occur
>     f = the number of outcomes or results favorable to the occurrence of that event
>     N = the total number of equally possible outcomes or results[6]

But what happens when complicated parameters are introduced, matrices are developed, or when more advanced studies are completed?

## ■ COST-OF-LOSS FORMULA

One of the indices used to study crime, natural catastrophe, and terrorism-based phenomena is the *cost-of-loss formula.* In this formula, variables are considered to discover how many "profits" certain types of incidents cost.

What would a hostage-taking incident cost you in terms of dollars? The cost-of-loss formula was originally used in a business environment, so theft is easily accounted for in this formula. Any business organization could use this formula to indicate the financial consequences of an airplane theft. If the plane could not be replaced quickly, the organization may be forced to cease operations in that area of the world and the theft would be "fatal."

If we take the "worst case" position and analyze each security vulnerability in light of the probable maximum loss if the risk event should occur under typical circumstances, we can use the following (criticality) formula:

$$K = (Cp + Ct + Cr + Cd - [I - a])$$

where :   K = criticality
C = cost
p = permanent replacement
t = temporary replacement
r = total related costs
d = discounted cash cost
I = available insurance or indemnity
a = allocable insurance premium amount

The formula can be applied to thefts, arson, kidnaping, and other risks, as well. The discounted cash cost can be eliminated, as well as the insurance information, if the asset loss is a human being.

The criticality formula also gives an assessment rating on how serious the impact of a terrorist encounter will be on the organization. If an attack were fatal, this would mean that the organization could go bankrupt or have to leave the country. These are the assessment ratings:

1. Fatal
2. Very Serious
3. Moderately Serious
4. Relatively Unimportant, and
5. Seriousness Unknown.[7]

The ratings can also be given numerical values for use in drawing charts, scales, grafts, or matrices. A fatal rating has a higher number than an activity that was judged as relatively unimportant.

To lower the financial aspects of risk in dangerous lands, many businesses now use kidnap/ransom insurance coverage. This insurance can be a real advantage, especially if the loss of a particular executive or owner would be fatal to the business. The coverage does have its limitations, however. Kidnap/ransom insurance is very expensive coverage. If you had a $250,000 kidnap policy on Mr. Smith, the insurance company will not pay your organization the premium at the time Mr. Smith is abducted. The insurance company will only refund the negotiated settlement or the amount of money you were able to raise from your own resources.

# ■ ENVIRONMENT

Environment has a tremendous influence on a crime. We have revolutionaries in the United States, but these groups have always failed in our very open, progressive, and established democracy. There are simply too many viable political alternatives to legitimate grievances, to select violence as a consistent method of dealing with conflict.

There are many environments, however, that significantly influence the safety of an expatriate organization—the physical environment, the political environment, the economic environment, and the social environment.

There are also other variables to consider in analyzing environments. One is the level of sophistication of those in power; another is the training, skill, and discipline of the police or military authority. Another variable is the expertise of the officer cadre of the local police or military organization. There may also be a historical experience. Certain lands have an extensive history of revolutionary behavior. It is almost an expected custom for young people and young adults to be involved in revolutionary activities in some parts of the world. If you are not a freedom fighter in certain areas, you may be looked down upon just as draft-dodgers may have been held in disdain during America's wars.

The variables of each local environment will not be specifically enumerated here. Population mix, population distribution, the average age of a population, the educational level of a population, the income level of a population, and the availability of viable employment opportunities in a population are very important variables. While employment opportunities are always strong variables in a violence-prediction index, the employment of university and technical school graduates is the most important of all, as most terrorists and revolutionary leaders are student leaders or recent graduates. These former students are especially dangerous in an economic milieu where there are no jobs for them. They went to colleges, technical schools, and universities to obtain a better way of life. They dreamed of a successful future. When they cannot get professional employment, even in entry-level positions, they become bitter. Their bitterness intensifies when they cannot even find a blue-collar job. They may become quite cynical and even desperate from their job-hunting revelations.

# ■ EVALUATE THE THREAT

The first step in risk assessment is to begin obtaining and collating threat data. Immediately upon beginning this task, you will encounter a dilemma. What is *good information?* How do you detect *bad information?* Is there a method whereby you can weigh the quality of your information?

Your sources will come primarily from your host government, your own embassy representatives, the media, law enforcement authorities, and national citizens that you trust. You must ascertain the quality of secondary information, as this information is opinion based on perceptions and beliefs. If these opinions are biased, uninformed, or emotionally reactive, then they can become very bad sources of information.

The business organization should have a method of evaluating the quality of information for accuracy and credibility. You can evaluate the credibility of your intelligence unit by ascertaining whether their futuristic projections came to pass. You should give a high level of credibility and weigh the source appropriately who gives you an accurate forecast on contemporary trends and events. Credibility is further increased when your source's predictions are consistently accurate.

Sources should be cultivated as a part of the planning process before a crisis occurs. If your organization has not accomplished this, do not throw up your hands in defeat. Go find some good sources, now! If you are in the middle of an emergency, ask the security officer or the representative of the Citizens Bureau at your Embassy for reliable sources with established track records.

You should also use the media. Listen to the radio—the BBC, The Voice of America Broadcasting Network, and the United States Armed Forces Radio and Television Network may be of real utility. Local television, radio, and the printed media may also be useful. This may continue to be true even if the news is slanted toward the Left, the Right, or toward a moderate stance. The reports can average themselves as you continue to accumulate and examine them.

You may find that there are news blackouts on terrorist events. This may even be the official policy of the government of your host country. The government policy of many developing nations is to ignore the existence and the threat of terrorism insofar as the mass media is concerned. This policy may be useful to the government in limiting the multiple benefits to terrorists, but it is quite limiting insofar as safety and counter-terrorism measures are concerned. You must know what your problem is before you take any countermeasures, evasive action, or a defensive stance. You must know enough about the events to believe that your counter-measures will be reasonably effective.

## ■ BUSINESS RISK ANALYSIS

Probably the best intelligence analysis material available in dangerous lands will come from western business organizations. They must know the real risk factor in order to stay in business. It is a wonderful opportunity if a security specialist at one of these multinational organizations will share information with you. Remember, though, that any information you receive will probably involve a reciprocal agreement. There may be some way *you* can help *them*. If there is, they will want you as a primary or secondary resource. A secondary resource would repeat rumor or private conversations. A primary source reports what she personally witnessed.

As you receive information, evaluate the source, evaluate the information, and evaluate the consequences if the information you hear is very important. It is important if the information reflects an unacceptable risk and the weighted score gives the information a high level of credibility. Always remember that the one who needs the information the most, is often the least likely to hear it.

## ■ RATE YOUR INFORMATION

Once you begin receiving information, you will want to assign a reliability factor to it. Reliable information from a source who has given accurate reports in the past should be given the highest ratings. Information from someone you do not know well should be given a much lower rating.

Information should be evaluated and rated using the following reliability index:

1. Very Reliable
2. Reliable
3. Unknown
4. Suspect Information
5. Unreliable Information

Very reliable information "makes sense" and can be verified by a quality source of information. Reliable information is consistent with your expectations. It originates with a reliable source and it is not in conflict with other information you receive from other reliable sources. Suspect information comes from someone you do not know well or perhaps you know the source well enough to question her credibility. Suspect information usually cannot be corroborated by a reliable source. If a terrorist group is maliciously spreading disinformation, you may find that multiple sources of questioned reliability are spreading the same rumor. Question any information that does not "fit" expectations. Unreliable information, on the other hand, may simply come from a source that you do not trust. Unreliable information is often contradicted by other sources and it can only rarely be verified.

Many authorities attempt to portray information graphically by horizontal and vertical axes intersecting at a midpoint. The vertical axis indicates the assessed reliability of the information; the horizontal axis indicates the assessed reliability of the source of information (see Figure 10.1).

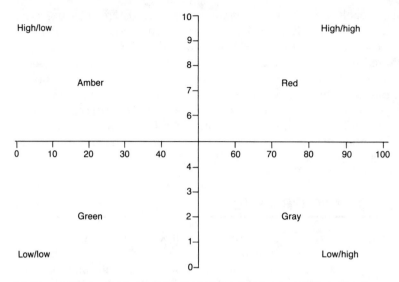

■ **Figure 10-1**   Crisis Plotting Grid Reprinted by permission of publisher, from CRISIS MANAGEMENT: PLANNING FOR THE INEVITABLE © 1986 Steven Fink. Published by AMACOM, a division of American Management Association, New York. All rights reserved.

Figure 10.1 has been adapted from Steven Fink's book on crisis management. The specifics were adopted for application to international business problems.

# ■ THE PROBABILITY FACTOR

Based on past experience and your knowledge of the situation, assess the percentage of the likelihood of the crisis occurring. There will be a percentage range of scores—0% is totally impossible, while 100% is an absolute or dead-certain possibility.

# ■ A COST ANALYSIS

You may also want to determine the cost of intervention. In many instances, the cost of countermeasures may be too expensive to pursue. You certainly would not want to spend $500 to prevent a potential $100 loss. Ask yourself, your family, and your organizations three questions:

1. How much would proactive intervention cost?
2. How much would reactive intervention cost?
3. How much will it cost me if I do not do anything?

## CRISIS IMPACT VALUE WORKSHEET

Rate the following questions on a 1–10 scale:

1. How intense might the crisis get?

   INTENSITY = (     )

2. How quickly might that happen?

   QUICKNESS = (     )

3. How much attention will the crisis draw to the organization?

   SCRUTINY = (     )

4. To what extent would the crisis intervene with your normal operation?

   DISRUPTION = (     )

5. What is the possible negative impact on the public image or the public perception of the organization?

   DAMAGE = (     )

6. To what extent would the crisis influence the ability of the organization to fulfill its mission?

   COST = (     )

   Total the scores: _____

   Divide the Total by 6: _____

The result is the Crisis Impact Value (CIV): _____

Now, tabulate your loss potentials and determine the most obvious and efficient course of action. Decide on whether it is worth intervening. Can you afford to intervene? Can you afford not to?

These methods show several prodromal indicators for your business-people and the organization itself. These methods, when professionally applied, can help indicate real problem areas and concerns. You can ignore those that are not really dangerous and pay special attention to those that are highly probable.

## ■ REFERENCES

1. Robert C. Klamser, "Crisis Management: A Crossroads for Law Enforcement" (an unpublished paper presented to the P.O.S.T. Command College, May 1988), 16.
2. Patrick Collins, *Living In Troubled Lands* (Boulder, CO: Paladin Press, 1981), 35.
3. Ibid., 36.

4. John M. Carroll, *Managing Risk: A Computer Aided Strategy* (Stoneham, MA: Butterworth Publishers, 1984), xv.

5. Ibid., xv.

6. Richard J. Healy and Timothy J. Walsh, *The Asset Protection Manuals* (Santa Monica, CA: The Merritt Company, 1989), 2–4.

7. Timothy J. Walsh and Richard J. Healy, *Protection of Assets Manual* (Santa Monica, CA: The Merritt Company, 1990), 2–16.

# 11

## ■ ■ BEGIN PLANNING NOW

While no one would want to become pessimistic, the recent accounts of businessperson hostage-taking, assault, rape, and murder are indicative of an apparent trend. More international businesspersons are being victimized than ever before and more types of businesses and service organizations are being targeted by criminals and terrorists. An appropriate response should be made and this initiative should come from within the business community.

The first step is to analyze the problem. Should anything be done? The second step includes devising an organizational policy. The third step is to develop a specific plan to handle the events that may confront many businesspeople and expatriates. The last step is to publish the policies and the plans and distribute them to all appropriate offices and individuals. Careful planning should precede any other response, policy initiative, or procedural counteraction.

There must be a plan—and it should be a good one—but any plan is only the first step. *Any* forethought gives a more appropriate response than a seat-of-the-pants reaction. It is very difficult to plan for unusual events that are outside the range of normal logic or understanding, but organizations that do not plan to *confront* crises will *react* to them.

## ■ AVOID INAPPROPRIATE ACTION

A reaction is normally not of the same quality as a planned confrontation. When there is no plan, a crisis reaction may be totally inappropriate. Further difficulties follow when there is no reaction agenda.

Some organizations seem to be reacting constantly to crisis situations. The original crisis may now be secondary to *created crises,* as the management team does the wrong things continuously. The old cliché that any reaction followed vigorously is better than no reaction at all, is a myth. To do the wrong thing or the right thing at the wrong time is detrimental in any crisis. In a crisis involving a revolutionary movement, an action of this type can be catastrophic. Human life can be lost by those who are not prepared to meet a terrorist agenda.

The organizations that react inappropriately, respond in this manner because there is no plan, no policy, or no real forethought. In the American business community, organizations have been held liable for their lack of preparation. The possibility of legal liability and responsibility should be carefully evaluated, just as there is a moral or organizational responsibility to prepare for danger.

# ■ HOW TO PLAN

Each corporation should decide how it will handle the planning process. The plans should fit the normal operational procedures accepted by each organization. Normally, the first step is for the CEO to call in top policy-makers. The security director, intelligence personnel, risk assessment managers, and the legal staff should outline the multiple-faceted risks facing the corporations management group.

The threat can be outlined in terms of all international work. Labor relation problems, revolutionary attacks, and extortion threats against the corporation are reviewed. The corporate risk analysts and intelligence personnel also indicate the probability of threats and violence in the future. The legal staff should also outline the corporation's liability if nothing is done, or if corporate responses result in tragedy.

Oftentimes, it is the legal aspect of corporate responsibility that moves an organization towards the development of policy and the implementation of specific plans and programs to deal with terrorism. Perhaps the best known American lawsuit was that of *Curtis* vs. *Beatrice Foods** filed in New York State in March of 1978. The Curtis case was quite broad in its claims, but it documented significant corporate negligence. The suit was also quite complicated in that the judge allowed the use of American law and Colombian labor and civil codes to document the plaintiffs position.

Even under ancient common law principles, a corporation has the responsibility to warn an employee of an impending potential threat, and to protect the employee. The issue of actual damages and punitive damages is separate from this basic tenet of law.

Some companies have discovered that the financial risk of doing nothing to warn or protect its employees in a threatening environment is quite expensive. Perhaps it is our lawyers, even more than our security, intelligence, and risk assessment personnel who have influenced corporate decision-making in this area.

The first step in the planning process requires the organization to make a policy or policies; or to accept the financial and legal risks of failing to make a policy. The second step is to decide what the corporate reaction

---

*481 F. Supp. 1275 [S.D.N.Y. 1980, *aff'd,* 633 F. 2d 203 (2d Cir. 1980)].

should be to terrorism. Then that reaction should be specified in a policy document or policy manual.

Once the policies are in place, the original planning group, or a second group of lower level managers, should get down to working on the basic strategies and tactics. Normally documents describing a Crisis Management Team (CMT) will be amended or approved by the CEO and will be then forwarded to all appropriate parties.

Sometimes the policy documents or the plans precede other stages of corporate activity. The training of CMT members and individual corporate members may now be necessary for the implemented policies, procedures, and plans to work well.

## ■ QUALITY CRISIS MANAGEMENT PLANNING

Professional, quality crisis management can be promptly implemented in any event for which a pre-crisis plan has been formulated. Quality crisis management can be conducted in those cases where a crisis manager has been trained to do the right things at the right time. Conversely, she has been trained to avoid accomplishing the wrong things or the right things in the wrong order. Timing is of critical importance in many man-made crisis situations.

The planning should be well documented and any training commensurate with the planning should be recorded. These measures will keep your organization out of the courtroom at some point in the future. You will be able to prove that your organization planned, provided training, and reacted from a policy guideline.

Governments, businesses, and humanitarian organizations, serving populations living in areas where violence is a way of life, should have normative standard operational plans (SOPs) for dealing with a terrorist crisis. *The worst time to prepare for a crisis is after it has already occurred!* Advance preparation can guarantee that crisis management does not bring your entire organization to a standstill. You will not lose sight of your normal organizational duties as you attempt to solve the crisis. Advance planning diminishes the overall impact of the crisis.

## ■ PLANNING FOR POLITICAL VIOLENCE

Planning for political violence is apparently a recent practice among many business organizations. The recurrence of terrorist problems has primarily occurred within the last three decades. Even when terroristic violence was a way of life, it was normally directed against legitimate government forces or national citizens. Expatriates and travelers were pretty much exempt unless they got caught in the cross fire by accident. Private businesses and humanitarian agencies were immune from almost all problems of this type in years past. While crime has always been a problem to the international businessperson, its prevalence has increased during the last decade. Except for the problems of evacuation during warfare, death, or illness, the typical business operation is rarely prepared to confront terroristic emergencies.

## ■ PLAN YOUR TRAINING

Many international business organizations have exceptional credentials in specialty areas. Their representatives are graduates of business colleges, universities, language schools, and cultural study centers. Many organizations have their own training courses to help their recruits succeed in their area of service.

It was perhaps the U.S. Peace Corps that gave the best cultural sensitivity training. Today there are many texts, manuals, videotapes, and audio cassettes available for purchase on this subject. These may assist even the small business organization in preparing for international service.

The major concerns of members of a business organization or humanitarian service representatives are terrorism and kidnapping insofar as emergencies and crisis management procedures are concerned. I confirmed this fact in my 1986 survey. Kidnapping by terrorists or criminals is also the concern most often voiced by expatriates living in dangerous lands. The material covered in this text addresses the issues that concerned the expatriates initially queried and interviewed.

## ■ WHAT SHOULD YOU PLAN FOR?

> Any measure that plans in advance for a crisis . . . any measure that removes the risk and uncertainty from a given situation . . . is indeed a form of crisis management.[1]

Contingency Preparation Consultants' spokesman Robert Klamser has this to say about planning for a crisis:

> Contingency planning is a process in which potential risks faced by an individual, family, or organization are identified and prioritized as to their likelihood of occurrence and degree of import. As a final step, plans are developed to deal with the risk.[2]

There *must* be a plan. Many business and humanitarian organizations have developed excellent approaches to evacuation in times of war or natural disaster. Some have also dealt with issues relating to life-threatening illness, the death of a family member back home, or administrative difficulties within a host country. Terrorism, guerrilla activity, and violent crime should also be included in the subjects covered in a standard organizational operation program. Unfortunately, many business and humanitarian organizations do not believe that they will become crisis casualties.

# ■ PRELIMINARY PLANNING

The planning group that develops the organizational crisis response policy should create a CMT as a part of that policy. The CMT members should be selected by position rather than by personalities; the team must be made up of hardworking individuals who have the ability to get along under the most arduous and stressful of conditions.

The CMT can then train together before an event ever occurs. Scenarios are especially useful in this training, since it helps the team member in conceptualizing the event before it occurs.

There is a tremendous stress associated with the threat of real danger and the potential loss of life associated with any terroristic encounter. But the organization with a plan has made a commitment to lower stress. They have increased the probability that the event will be handled in a competent and professional manner. The CMT should be formally recognized as an integral part of the organizational structure.

What can your organization do? What should it do? Several business organizations have lamented the fact that they were ill-prepared to cope, much less deal professionally or successfully, with these types of crises. There must be a good, simple strategy to deal with any emergency. The development of a response plan is the key to the successful recovery of an abduction victim. This plan may be the most important element in saving someone's life (perhaps yours) at a later date.

Any policy and any plan should be written and published within the organization. One good rule of thumb to follow in a contingency plan is to assume that the worst (or weakest) possible person will be the only one available at the time the crisis develops. Assume that none of the best managers from your organization will be available to help with the emergency during the initial stages of its development. Therefore, the plan should be written in such a way that even the most emotional employee will be able to comprehend it. It should have numbered lists of things to do, such as (1) Call your superior; (2) Call the home office; (3) Call the Security Department. The document should enable *anyone* to follow the plan. There is no room for misunderstandings. Some organizational specialists use the *KISS Principle* to deal with complicated agendas—Keep It Simple, Stupid.

The first step in conceiving a working plan is to give particular personnel the responsibility for designing the crisis management plan. There needs to be a very clear executive-level decision delineating the responsibility for the design of a plan and for actualizing the plan should the organization confront an emergency.

After a kidnapping has occurred in a remote region of the world is the worst possible time to have an organizational dispute over who is in charge or responsible for the resolution of the problem. If clear lines of responsibility are carefully prescribed in the plan, then a spontaneous and appropriate reaction to the problem can be implemented quickly. A policy manual resulting from the initial planning stage is really helpful for the CMT. The organization's response should now be smooth, articulate, and precise.

The act of planning will also reduce the stress and anxiety levels of all concerned. It suddenly becomes acceptable to talk about the unacceptable. Most employees will not discuss their fears in a conventional setting, but the organization can create an environment in which it is all right to discuss these very real fears and concerns. Planning also ensures that many of the potential unknown factors will be reviewed prior to encountering them in an actual hostage event or terrorist encounter. The planning stage is a pre-developmental tool for a future support system from within the resources of the organization. The mere act of planning builds confidence. The organization's members now feel better able to respond in a crisis.

Knowing what to expect will really assist the victim. He can maintain his composure and does not have to wonder what is happening back at the office. With training, policies and a procedural manual he has, in effect, a *terrorism tool kit*. If the contingency plans include a viable training program, then the victim can feel confident in knowing that every reasonable effort is being accomplished to resolve the situation. "A few hours, or even minutes, spent considering the possible consequences of a terrorist attack can have tremendous benefits as is shown by the numerous reports of those who have been held hostage."[3]

> The plan is nothing more than a tool to enable you to solve the crisis. However, the better your crisis management plan, the better your tools. And superior tools in the hands of a skilled artificer will go a long way toward insuring opportunity instead of danger.[4]

# ■ TERRORISM DECISIONMAKING

Under crisis conditions, the manager has relatively little time to analyze available alternatives (her own or those of an adversary) or to develop new capabilities. A crisis presents the decision-maker with many agonizing management choices. Even in planning, the manager has a Pandora's Box of alternative decisions. Some of the questions a manager should ask are

What would the Corporation have me do?
Which is the best decision?
What should be my priority at this time?
What can *I* do?
What can my *organization* do?

Some organizations accept the officially stated policy of the United States Government, which is

No negotiations.
No compromise.
No concessions.
No ransom.

Yet we find that most American business organizations do pay ransom— it seems to be the cost of doing business in many host countries. Several hundred million dollars have been paid in ransoms during the last decade. Indeed, in one single incident, the Exxon Oil Company paid $14.2 million for the release of Victor Samuelson in Argentina.

# ■ SPECIFIC CRISIS PLANS

By definition, a plan is a documentation of a projected course of action or a desired future state of affairs. There are long-range plans, short-range plans, strategic plans, and tactical plans. Short-range plans often tend to have relatively inflexible goals. Long-range plans have more flexible goals, but are generally not so well-defined on a procedural level. Strategic plans include the major goals and objectives of the international organization. Tactical plans include structured and detailed planning on narrowly defined problems. Tactical plans are usually short-range in nature and deal with a specific task, problem, or issue. Through careful planning, an organization can be well prepared to meet most adversarial challenges from a professional and proactive posture.

The book *Crisis Management: Planning for the Inevitable* capsulizes an ancient Greek concept. Steven Fink, the author, discusses the *prodromal stage* of a crisis. The term is derived from the Greek word *prodrome* and is best translated as meaning running before. In effect, a prodrome is a warning sign or a pre-crisis indicator. Surely the prodromals exist today for business organizations and the humanitarian agency community. Being aware of the prodrome allows us to be more vigilant, to be more prepared, to plan in advance for contingencies that may be reasonably expected.

Planning reduces many of the unknowns. The committee that designs or implements a policy or a specific action or reaction has carefully considered the crisis stage of a problem. They have thought through the crisis stages, at least to some degree. Any planning is superior to none. A real commitment is necessary for all planning committee participants. Superficiality is inappropriate and inadequate while preparing for a reasonably probable crisis, especially when the prodromals are well-articulated.

Planning also provides an open forum for dealing with crisis issues. Many businesspeople may have broadly variant philosophical concepts guiding their attitudes over the multiple issues of dealing with terrorism. Many have accepted the recommendations of our own State Department of no concessions, no compromises, no negotiations, and no ransoms. However, the Iran-Contra hearings revealed that our government has consistently responded to extortion demands—but behind closed doors and beyond public scrutiny.

Dr. Neil Livingston wrote a recent book entitled *The Complete Security Guide for Corporate Executives* in which he focuses on the improbability of terrorist attacks against Americans, but added a caveat.

> The ordinary American's chances of being killed or injured in a terrorist attack or being taken hostage are relatively slim. Calculated from the actuarial tables, the average American's chances of being killed in a terrorist attack are less than the possibility of accidental death due to a fall, being struck by lightning, poisoning, fire, a motor vehicle crash, and virtually every other category of accidental death for which the U.S. Public Health Service keeps figures. If you are a diplomat, a member of the military, or a corporate executive in some parts of the world, however, your chances of being killed in a terrorist attack rise significantly, and you should adopt certain precautions to minimize your risk.[5]

Planning also provides an opportunity for the members of each organization to have an assigned role and responsibility. When the planning is taking place within the family unit, the context is the same. Each family member will have a job to accomplish should catastrophe strike. This, too, decreases stress as each participant knows what to do and knows what others are doing.

If captors harass the victim with statements like "we will take your family next," the captive is already in a position to know that the family has been moved to a safe haven and thus removed from danger. Harassing tactics will then be totally unsuccessful.

## ■ GOOD—BETTER—BEST

Planning results in better decisions, actions, and reactions during a critical incident. Invariably, these advance decisions will be better than those made under duress during the midst of a crisis. The organization, too, will have multiple responses to prepare for the victim's family, the host government, the home government, friends, and the media.

The business organization has a legal, moral, and ethical responsibility to respond appropriately during a crisis. Advance research, careful preparation, group thinking, and concise planning will all assist an organization in developing an appropriate response pattern. In private businesses, there have been many successful civil suits towards organizations that were not prepared for terrorism. The victims have sued the corporation and, in one incident, a wife sued the corporation while her husband was still in captivity. An organization that has established policies relating to terrorism, as well as specific plans to deal with terrorism, is less likely to be successfully addressed in a lawsuit.

Finally, there is a need, not only to deal with the crisis, but a need for the organization to get on with their primary business. Many organizations spend the majority of their administrative energies in dealing with a terroristic event. Had the organization prepared before the crisis, they could have gotten on with their normal work operations much more expeditiously.

The time to meet governmental officials, intelligence officers, police administrators, and hostage rescue unit coordinators is *before* the incident occurs. These pre-formed relationships can save countless hours of ill-timed preparation. Area businesspeople should get to know the embassy or consular security officers. Keep the lines of communication open during perilous times. This should be an ongoing relationship, not just a single contact. Any pre-formed contacts are better than none at all.

Planning and programmed development of pre-formed relationships can help prevent the organizational disruption that is often one of the primary terrorist motivations. Contingency planning is appropriate, necessary, and vital. It is not a substitute for common sense. A contingency plan provides a foundation for a systematic and structured response and reaction. The plan provides specific answers tailored to fit actual crisis situations. Terrorists attempt to keep the business organization off balance in all reactions so they may interject unexpected demands or tensions.

The key to resolving a crisis remains within the plan. We need to study indigenous and international terror organizations. We must think and reason with the best available information and training that we have. We must apply the principles of planning to actual events, as they occur.

# ■ REFERENCES

1. Richard Cole, *Executive Security: A Corporate Response to Abduction and Terrorism* (New York: Wiley Interscience, 1980), 75.
2. Robert Klamser, "Missionary Hostage? What Will Your Agency Do?" *Evangelical Missionary Quarterly* 24 (1) (January 1988): 31.

3. Robert H. Kupperman and Darrel M. Trent, *Terrorism: Threat, Reality and Response* (Stanford: Hoover Institution Press, 1979), 226.
4. Steven Fink, *Crisis Management: Planning for the Inevitable* (New York: American Management Association, 1986), 66.
5. Neil C. Livingston, *The Complete Security Guide for Corporate Executives* (Lexington, MA: Lexington Books, 1989), 16.

# 12

## ■■ INDIVIDUAL AND FAMILY PLANS

What should you do for yourself? What should you do for your family? Does your family have a plan? Is the plan well thought out? Is there a follow-up to ensure preparedness? *You are responsible for your own security and that of your family! No one else can accept it.* No one else will. An organizational crisis manager stationed in the U.S. is not gong to help much during the beginning phases of your overseas crisis. If you want to be prepared, start designing your plan now. The person best equipped to prevent your crisis is you. If you follow the tenets of crime and terrorism avoidance, your potential crisis may be over before it begins. If you fail to observe, avoid, or prevent, your personal safety is still up to you.

If you are suddenly in the middle of a crisis, such as a revolution or massive earthquake, you need to make some decisions. If you have planned as an individual and with your family, you are already equipped to make informed choices.

## ■ PLANS FOR LEAVING THE COUNTRY

In some instances, it may be best to leave the country, at least for a short time. If there is a revolution or a war, your family may be in unnecessary danger. In some instances, there may be problems associated with obtaining rations such as food, gasoline, medicine, or safe drinking water.

In emergencies, many expatriates flee to the nearest airport. Driving or walking to the airport may be incredibly dangerous. In the fall of the Democratic Republic of the Congo in 1964, more than 2800 expatriates were killed—many of them were rounded up at the Stanleyville Airport by the Simbas. Only the intrusion of irregular troops and mercenaries kept the death tolls as low as they were. During the Simba Revolution, many expatriates literally hiked to safety. They crossed the border of one country and went into an adjacent nation. A good individual or family plan in a situation like this would be to

**1.** have a pre-planned and established route of departure. Keep maps ready in order to develop alternative routes should this process become necessary.

**2.** have a readily available supply of cash on hand. Use it as necessary for the emergency.

**3.** have your knapsacks or suitcases packed and ready for an emergency evacuation. When or if the situation really gets bad, you want to be able to leave on a moment's notice.

**4.** store basic items in a hidden location. This cache may include food, clothing, bottled water, and fuel. Sometimes, expatriates who are widely dispersed from each other have previously agreed to meet at the cache for a multifamily, joint evacuation effort during a time of crisis.

**5.** establish a location where families will meet should they become separated.

Coping with a crisis period requires a lot of forethought. Specific plans and policies can help immensely, but they need to be well thought out. Some organizations have a formal or informal policy against the payment of gifts, bribes, or gratuities of any form. While this is normally a reasonable business policy, insofar as moral, ethical, and legal constraints are concerned, it may not be good strategy during a time of crisis.

Suppose you are faced with a massive aerial evacuation of expatriates and the higher-status personnel of the host country. This situation can be a nightmare. Perhaps four to five times more passengers are attempting to depart than is normally the case. You may find that even if you already have confirmed tickets for a specific flight, you may have difficulty getting on the plane. During an emergency, new tickets may be issued at your local airport. Note that your final confirmation may be contingent upon a "gift" to your ticket agent. The realization of this contingency could save your life. You cannot assume that you will get a seat on the next flight out of the country. Normal flight routines may not be followed.

In dealing with this type of contingency, your best bet is to plan for alternative methods of leaving the country. By having carry-on luggage only, you can literally walk to safety in many instances. In some cases, this plan is not feasible. Perhaps you are too centrally located or your "walk" is several hundred miles. If this is the case, you may consider a *drive-out*, as many westerners recently accomplished while evacuating Iraq and Kuwait. If you have a sturdy vehicle, such as a four-wheel drive automobile or truck, you may be able to drive away from the main roads to cross international borders.

You can never assume anything in regard to evacuating a country, especially in another culture. What if one spouse needs to take the children back home? In some cultures, this exit could present many difficulties. If the spouse who is not returning stateside is present at the airport or dock, then the problems associated with departure are lessened. But if one spouse is a hostage victim or unavailable for travel, the host country enforcement officials may not allow one parent to leave with the children. Your embassy staff may be able to help you deal with this event, but a power-of-attorney statement can be critical in obtaining approval to leave the country. A power-of-attorney statement that has been processed through the legal system of the host country can solve many problems. In some cases, both husband and wife can appear before a local magistrate and authorize the other spouse to take the children out of the country.

The countries that require *both* parents to escort their children out of the country are trying to prevent parental kidnapings and illegal deportations. They should be applauded for their efforts in this regard. You should, however, be aware of this possibility and should make preparations to leave long before any emergency situation develops. Keep a Rapid Evacuation Checklist (REC) available so that you will not overlook an essential item or activity (see page 132).

In some cases, evacuees abandon cars, homes, apartments, and furnishings. If you are planning to return for your valuables, have a local friend or business associate house-sit to keep your losses to a minimum.

## ■ BOMB THREATS

History shows that bombing is by far the most common type of terrorism and you should be prepared for this event. Assume that you are at home or at the office and you receive a bomb threat. The caller claims to represent the National Liberation Front (NLF). "You have been targeted," the caller states, "and even now a bomb is located in your building." What should you do? What should you *not* do? Preparation is the key to reducing the damage that a bomb can do.

A bomb threat is a very serious issue. Over fifty percent of all terrorist attacks are in the form of bombings. Many western businesses and your embassy or consular officer may have bomb detection equipment or explosive detection dogs. Even if they do, and use them, a careful visual search should be made of buildings and grounds by someone familiar with the facility. High-level plastic explosives are difficult to discover. A very small bomb with high-tech explosives can do a lot of damage. Bomb detection equipment usually detects dynamite, TNT, firebombs, and other primitive explosives. These explosives emit a vapor that is easily detectable by a vapor measuring unit or a well-trained explosive detection dog. Unfortunately, the new plastic or plastique explosives emit only a very slight vapor that cannot always be detected by dogs or other devices.

If you are in a location in which you may be accosted with a bomb threat,

## RAPID EVACUATION CHECKLIST

PERSONAL ITEMS
- Passports        Location:_____
- Visas        Location:_____
- Health records        Location:_____
- Family records        Location:_____
- Photographs        Location:_____
- _____        Location:_____
- _____        Location:_____
- _____        Location:_____
- _____        Location:_____
- _____        Location:_____

FINANCIAL ITEMS
- Bankbook        Location:_____
- Checkbook        Location:_____
- Credit cards        Location:_____
- Financial records        Location:_____
- Cash        Location:_____
- _____        Location:_____
- _____        Location:_____
- _____        Location:_____
- _____        Location:_____
- _____        Location:_____
- _____        Location:_____

ORGANIZATION-RELATED ITEMS
- Employee records        Location:_____
- Translations        Location:_____
- Property records        Location:_____
- Confidential records        Location:_____
- _____        Location:_____
- _____        Location:_____
- _____        Location:_____
- _____        Location:_____

OTHER ITEMS
- _____        Location:_____
- _____        Location:_____
- _____        Location:_____
- _____        Location:_____
- _____        Location:_____
- _____        Location:_____
- _____        Location:_____
- _____        Location:_____
- _____        Location:_____

it is necessary to develop an emergency evacuation plan. If you have an evacuation plan for fire and natural disaster, it may be appropriate to use the same scheme for a bomb threat.

By rehearsing the evacuation plan, you may prevent panic in the event of a real threat. The plan should name the person who will make the decision to evacuate the area and should designate specific personnel to take charge. Alternates must be designated, as well, so that someone in authority will always be available to manage the evacuation. Terrorists may want you to evacuate, therefore you need to ensure the safety of your family and business associates upon their exit. Route them to a secure area. When security personnel, the police, or military authorities arrive, request security coverage until the incident is over.

When faced with a bomb threat, the number one priority is to prevent panic. Since there are many harassment calls of this type, the threat may not be legitimate. Even as you listen to the telephone threat, remember that only about 2% of reported bomb threats turn out to be valid.[1]

> There is no way of predicting whether a threat will be a thoughtless prank, an irresponsible ruse [to cover a servant's late return], a deliberate method of harassment designed to cause disruption or panic—or a warning of an impending explosion. But because of the potential risk of injury to persons are so high, few threats can be ignored.[2]

Bombs can be very "intelligent." They can be blown up by reaching a certain time, height, pressure, or temperature. They can be set off manually by a simple fuse, by a radio frequency (such as those used in garage door openers or some burglar alarms), or by a police radio transmission.

If you, your family, or a business associate gets a telephone threat, remember to stay calm; avoid panic. The telephone listener should try to keep the caller on the line. There is little that could be said to a bomb threat caller that could intensify or worsen the situation. After all, the caller has already threatened to kill you. The caller may state that the bomb has been set to go off within a specific time frame. *If it is a lie, you cannot change the deception.* If it is true, you probably do not have the skills necessary to stop the explosion, but there are some things you *can* do.

Listen to the caller; you can learn from what the caller says. In fact, the phone call may be used as a tool to defuse the situation. In some countries, the phone call can be traced. Get an associate to use another line to call the phone company or the police. The longer you keep the caller on the phone, the better. If possible, turn on a tape recorder to establish a permanent record of the event.

Whoever receives the call must ask the right questions. Ask where the bomb is located. This question can help you determine whether or not the bomb threat is a hoax. Ask the caller if the bomb is in a specific location and *name a place that does not exist.* If the caller says the bomb is at that location, then you know the threat is groundless. A "sweep" should still be made of the building for safety reasons. At the very least, the caller may reveal a location that gives security teams a place to begin their search.

The Bomb Threat Checklist is a good tool to use when faced with a threat (see page 135). Give it to your family members, your telephone exchange personnel, and your business associates. Leave copies in all employee residences.

All of these actions may not be necessary, although in some cases they may be. For instance, a secondary explosion from a gas leak could be worse than the primary detonation. Frayed electric wires could short and cause a fire after an explosion.

## ■ MAIL-IN BOMB THREATS

Some bomb threats are made by mail. This is especially true when the person making the threat is afraid that you will recognize her voice, trace the call, or that you use voice detection equipment.

Keep everything you receive in the mail that is related to the bomb threat. Keep the envelope and the written communication. Instruct the staff or family members who open the mail to put the letter and the envelope down immediately upon reading the threat. Do not touch the letter and envelope again. The police or embassy security personnel may be able to lift fingerprints from the paper using ninhydrin, super glue, or some other detection method.

If you receive a strange package or bulky envelope, leave it alone. *Do not open it.* If a package or envelope feels sticky or greasy, *do not open it!* If you are not expecting a package from a vendor, then do not accept it unless you telephone to determine the appropriateness of the delivery. Simple safety measures like these can save your life.

## ■ FAMILY PLANS FOR KIDNAPING

Many of the policies and emergency plans that an organization makes apply to the family. Some organizations now require dependents to leave the country at the time of a hostage-taking. This requirement is not an easy one—the wife may feel she is abandoning her husband and the children may prefer to stay near their father.

If the family policy is created around the needs of the potential victim, then the family should move. The victim will not be overly concerned about the family, if he knows that they are safe. This knowledge is of significant aid in helping the victim maintain his emotional equilibrium. The wife can always return to the host country if she happens to be needed.

## BOMB THREAT CHECKLIST

■ What TIME was the threat received?_____
■ What LINE/NUMBER was called?_____
■ WHEN will bomb detonate?_____
■ WHERE was the bomb placed?_____
■ HOW MANY bombs were placed?_____
■ WHY was the bomb placed there?_____
■ WHO (or what group) planted the bomb?_____
■ Was the caller MALE or FEMALE?_____
■ Guess the approximate AGE of the caller._____
  Adult?_____ Teenager?_____ Child?_____
■ EMOTIONAL STATE of the caller._____
  Calm?_____ Excited?_____ Angry?_____
■ Were there any BACKGROUND NOISES?_____
  Factory?_____ Train?_____ Ship?_____
  Traffic?_____ Marketplace?_____
■ Did you detect any ACCENT?_____
■ What was the probable NATIONALITY of the caller?_____
■ What was the probable ETHNIC BACKGROUND of the caller?
  _____
■ What was the RATE of speech of the caller?
  Fast?_____ Moderate?_____ Slow?_____
■ What was the VOLUME of the caller's voice?_____
  Loud?_____ Moderate?_____ Soft?_____
■ Were there any unique VOICE QUALITIES?_____
  Low?_____ Middle?_____ High?_____
■ Describe the caller's VOICE._____
  _____
■ Did the call sound like a LOCAL or LONG DISTANCE call?_____
■ Did the caller's voice sound FAMILIAR?_____
■ Did the caller ask for a PARTICULAR PERSON?_____
■ Write down what the CALLER SAID, *using his exact words,* if possible._____
  _____

Call Recipient's Actions After Receiving the Call._____
■ Call managers.
■ Call police.
■ Call military bomb disposal unit.
■ Call your Embassy or Consulate.
■ Call Fire Department.
■ Call ambulance service.
■ Call phone company.
■ Call electric company.
■ Call gas company.

In planning for contingencies, the whole family should be informed. Even young children should be taught what to do and what not to do. Both spouses should be thoroughly acquainted with all family business transactions. Bank account records, credit card billings, and the billing dates for all recurring expenses should be kept in a convenient and accessible location. Property deeds, vehicle titles, power-of-attorney statements, and emigration permission documents for dependent children should all be stored in an easily accessible location. An "emergency contact list" should also be maintained with up-to-date addresses and phone numbers. When a crisis develops, you can readily contact these people within a very short period of time. Identify particular police or military officials as the designated reporting authority. Interview them to discuss emergency procedures. These individuals can get the bureaucracy working for you quickly. Association with them can be of incalculable value.

# ■ MEDIA RELATIONSHIPS

Most organizations have established media policies when dealing with a crisis. Some family members, however, may feel that they are exceptions to this rule. There is a lot of pressure from reporters to get anyone to accept an interview. However, be aware that in a kidnapping or a major emergency, an impromptu interview can be dangerous and should be avoided. You do not know the context in which you will be quoted or misquoted. The CMT should be the only focal point for the media. If a release is necessary, the CMT can help spouses prepare for the interview by coaching them in appropriate remarks and informing them of any inappropriate subjects that should be avoided altogether.

# ■ REFERENCES

1. Paul Fuqua and Terry V. Wilson, *Terrorism: The Executives Guide to Survival* (Dallas: Gulf Publishers, 1978), 57.
2. Graham Knowles, *Bomb Security Guide* (Los Angeles: Security World Publishing Company, 1976), 47.

# 13

## ■■ FORMULATE POLICY

Policies should be established to assist those responsible for preparing plans. Crisis policy development is a prudent course of action in times of danger or potential danger. These policies should be designed to meet the intent and objectives of the CMT. Some organizations, for example, may have the policy to not react to the crisis. They plan to do nothing at all and will see what will work out. If a local plant manager is taken hostage, the organization would choose to do nothing, if that is their policy. Under any circumstance, it is imperative that the expatriate organization define its policy prior to a crisis event. To consider the formulation of policy while planning the specifics of how to react to an ongoing crisis may well create a quagmire of deliberations.

### ■ CORPORATE POLICY

If an organization has established a crisis policy, it is quite easy to expedite the assignments of individuals by position and rank, experience and maturity, or site location. Normally, the first policy decision would be to determine whether the organization will react to any crisis. If the organization is to react, then the policy should specify the particular organizational approach. A plan can then be developed to deal with the specifics of the event.

Many business organizations have accepted the "team" approach used by governmental, industrial, and military organizations to establish policy. Many business executive boards have committees that recommend specific policies to the board. In all the cases I reviewed, the formation of the CMT was of the first or highest priority.

The Headless Chicken Syndrome is encountered when there are no organizational policies to regulate the collective and individual activities of its members. Everyone feels that they must do something in a crisis. Unfortunately, "something" may be the wrong thing. A policy relating to a crisis will remove all doubt as to appropriate procedure or as to who is in charge. A policy will prevent the activities of an untrained individual who may not have the sensitivity, discretion, or knowledge appropriate to resolving the crisis. A simple public statement made by an untrained businessperson, such as "our organization will *never* pay a ransom demand," can get an associate killed. The trained crisis communicator *never says "no" and never says "never"* to a terrorist or criminal holding a gun at an associate's head. The trained communicator might say, "I know our organization has a policy against the payment of a ransom demand, but perhaps the family, concerned friends, or the victim's church, could raise a small ransom." A crisis policy saves lives by providing direction and saving time.

Your policy should stipulate who is authorized to release information for the organization. As stated in Appendix 2 of this document, the CMT Public Relations Officer is the only conduit for the release of official or unofficial information.

Your policy should also instruct members of the organization on how to forward information relevant to the crisis. Information is *always* forwarded to the CMT. Please note that Appendix 1 of this text contains a policy for crisis management. Briefly, the policy states that the Board of Directors gives the Chief Executive Officer (CEO) the authority to appoint the appropriate CMT and CMT Chairman. The CEO can make these appointments immediately upon notification of an incident.

The CEO is further authorized to bring in a crisis management consultant and a hostage negotiator if this action is appropriate. An "emergency" or "contingency fund" of $20,000 to $30,000 should be easily accessible if this action is recommended. The initial expenses of the CMT should be guaranteed. If the CMT members have already been trained in crisis management concepts (see Appendix 7), then they are immediately ready to get to work on the crisis.

The communications policy provided in Appendix 2 of this document prohibits a spouse from making public statements regarding the hostage situation. It also prohibits all employees from making these statements. Only the CMT is authorized to make public statements.

Unauthorized disclosure of hostage information can negate all negotiations. Let's examine a worst-case scenario. Suppose the CMT has just completed the negotiation for the safe release of a hostage. The terms have been completed, but the transfer has not yet occurred. The release agreement includes a required statement from the hostage stating that he has been treated well and humanely by "a group of freedom fighters seeking their liberation from governmental oppression."

In the midst of these delicate negotiations, perhaps even as the release agreement is being finalized, the expatriate wife is interviewed by the media. The wife says that she "is praying that the *criminals* who took her husband hostage will release him." Whoa! Wait a minute. The hostage-takers have an image problem; they want to be labeled as *freedom fighters* fighting for basic human rights in a repressive governmental regime. The hostage's wife just labeled them as common criminals.

The hostage who was about to be released will, most likely, not be released on schedule now. The delay from this one remark will last days or even weeks. The next negotiated release may require the wife to apologize for her statement. She may be forced to do this on radio, TV, and in the press.

Hostage negotiation matters must be handled diplomatically by trained negotiators and media specialists. Even some of the most distinguished diplomats occasionally err during this type of crisis. President Nixon and President Reagan have exacerbated ongoing hostage resolution events by their rhetoric.

President Reagan intensified the negotiations for the 39 remaining hostages of TWA Flight 847 in Beirut, Lebanon. Just as the ordeal seemed to be ending, Reagan was quoted as having made impromptu remarks at a political rally in Chicago.

Reagan had said that the hijackers were

> "murderers, thugs, and thieves." He said that there was no linkage to the Israeli release of Atlit prisoners [735 Shiites not currently charged with any crimes[1]] and the release of the Flight 847 Hostages. He seemed to warn of reprisals against the hijackers and their sponsors. "I don't think anything that attempts to get people back who have been kidnapped by thugs, murderers, and barbarians is wrong to do."
>
> The U.S. press was screaming that the rhetoric had scuttled the release and that the Hizbollah, widely believed to have planned and carried out the hijacking, were scared of air strikes and other retaliation.[2]

Another example of an off-the-cuff remark by a Chief Executive (President Richard Nixon) concerned two U.S. diplomats kidnapped and murdered in Khartoum.

> In 1973, Palestinian terrorists, members of Black September, took over the Saudi Arabian Embassy in Khartoum. In return for the release of other hostages, who included one Belgium and two American diplomats, the Ambassador and the Deputy Chief of Mission—the terrorists demanded, among other things, the release of the imprisoned assassin of Senator Robert Kennedy. For the first two days, the terrorists took no action. Sudanese officials informed them that a high-ranking American official, the Under Secretary of State, was on his way to Khartoum. Meanwhile, in the course of a routine press conference at the White House, reporters asked President Nixon if the United States was going to release Kennedy's killer. The President replied that the U.S. would never give in to terrorist blackmail. This comment was rebroadcast to Khartoum. The terrorists reportedly heard it on their radio. Shortly after that, they murdered the one Belgian and the two American hostages.[3]

President Nixon had a negotiator enroute to the incident, but the Palestinians probably believed that the actual U.S. political resolve was much lower than that stated by our elected Chief Executive. President Nixon also said "no" and "never." You do not say this to someone who is holding a gun to a hostage's head. You must buy time. Leaders must be deterred from speaking to the media on matters such as this until there is the opportunity to resolve the crisis.

President Reagan later referred to "thieves, murderers, and barbarians" holding Americans hostage. They were thieves—they stole nearly $750,000 in cash and valuables from the hostages. They were murderers—they had already killed Robert Dean Stetham, a diver in the U.S. Navy. Also, Stetham was cruelly mistreated before he was executed, so Reagan could legitimately say that these men were barbarians. But sometimes, telling the absolute truth is the worst thing that can be done. President Reagan's rhetoric cost the TWA 847 hostages another two days in captivity. The hostages would have been released sooner if the terrorists' "honor" had not been slandered. Those two extra days of hostage captivity would be critically reviewed today if a hostage had suffered a heart attack, a mental breakdown, or attempted to escape and was killed.

If two Presidents could err to this degree, think how easily an untrained family member or business associate could make a critical error of judgment in releasing a statement. Again, the CMT should issue all releases. The release should be written or read to reporters. Extemporaneous questions from reporters should not be answered.

# ■ POSTCRISIS POLICY

Some years ago, I was appointed as the Director of the second largest State Narcotics Investigation Agency in the United States. Upon accepting the position, I carefully examined the agency's *Policy and Procedure Manual*. I discovered that there were no policy requirements for post-shoot-out psychological consultation. There was no requirement that an agent receive counseling after killing a law violator or while protecting himself. As Director, I wrote the policy the first day and made the policy public during the second day of my appointment.

Before my first year in this position was over, a shooting death occurred. It was a justifiable shooting—the undercover agent drew and fired at an armed robber. The robber had already taken the agent's money and the agent had passively submitted to the robber. When the agent realized that he was to be killed, he drew his weapon and killed the robber. The post-shoot-out policy was enforced and the agent was required to see a psychologist. However, the agent was adamant in stating that he did not want to go—he did not need to "see a shrink." I made him go anyway.

Years later, the agent thanked me for the policy. He was still getting counseling. He needed it because he was still having flashbacks, daydreams, and nightmares about the event. In spite of the fact that this was a justifiable shooting, he felt very guilty about the man's death.

A businessperson who has been held hostage may react in the same way—"I don't need counseling. I'm all right. I am handling my problems just fine. Let me go back to work now." To apply the policy to *that* person is an arbitrary decision, perhaps even capricious, even if he or she desperately needs the counseling. It will be applied to an individual, not all individuals victimized in this way.

It is better to establish a non-stigmatizing post-trauma therapeutic session policy *before* anybody needs it. Your corporation can then apply the policy to the individual who fits the conditions stated within the policy. A well-written policy will require that *all* individuals who have been victimized in this type of traumatic event receive post-trauma counseling. Children, as well as other members of the extended family, may need therapy. CMT members and others who were under great stress during the event may also be included. After all, they were making life and death decisions. If anything went wrong, they probably would have assumed the blame—at least some of it, if not all. The policy should also mandate follow-up evaluations in 6- to 12-month intervals in order to evaluate repressed post-incident behavior.

## ■ HOSTAGE NEGOTIATION POLICY

The organization must decide on the negotiation policy. Perhaps it will decide not to negotiate. If so, this decision should be documented in a formal policy. The statement should be distributed to all those concerned. Debates over negotiation and non-negotiation are always intense and they will be doubly so when your co-worker is a victim. Decide on how you will handle the matter before it becomes an issue.

## ■ RANSOM PAYMENTS

If you decide to negotiate, you should establish a ransom policy. Remember that the terrorists may not demand money in exchange for their hostage. The Symbionese Liberation Army required that Randolph Hearst, the billionaire publisher, pay out more than $1,000,000 in milk and food products to poor people in a particular California ghetto. Intermediary social action groups were selected to ensure that only top-quality goods were dispensed.

Certainly, your business organization would not want to transfer large sums to fund guns, ammunition, and explosives. The business organization with philanthropic interests may, on the other hand, be quite willing and able to feed the hungry, clothe the naked, and provide water services and wells for those who are thirsty and live in arid lands. An organization may even be asked to locate and staff a school, a clinic, or a hospital in an area considered too dangerous in which to operate. You may even get a "protection guarantee" to go where you have wanted an assignment for years. You will never know unless you negotiate. You will never know unless you keep all doors of communication open and listen to all potentials and opportunities.

Sometimes, an incredibly small payment is acceptable to the hostage-taker. If you could pay an "expense payment" to the terrorists for safely maintaining and guarding your expatriate, would you do it? Many business organizations have capitulated to ransom payments when a human life is concerned. Some of these were token ransoms. In most cases, the payment was a violation of their written policy. Many businesses systematically accept the U.S. Government's stated policy, never realizing that the government has violated its own policy for at least three decades.

Perhaps the first diversion from policy occurred in 1973 when the U.S. Ambassador to Haiti was abducted. A $500,000 U.S. ransom was demanded. Francois Duvalier ("Papa Doc"), the President of Haiti, summoned French negotiators to expedite the release. Three days later, the Ambassador was released after Papa Doc personally paid an undisclosed ransom (generally believed to have been $175,000). Since massive U.S. aid was being poured into Haiti at the time, why should we kid ourselves over who really paid the ransom?

In setting up your ransom policy, make sure that you issue a policy that you can live with. Do not issue conservative directives that field representatives will not or cannot follow. Do not issue policies that will be purposely disregarded in the field. There must be a clear understanding of the policy. Appropriate plans may then be forthcoming.

# ■ POWER-OF-ATTORNEY AUTHORIZATION

Another matter to consider is the power-of-attorney authorization. In some ways, this policy may be more important than all of the others. To illustrate my point, I provide you with a scenario. All references are fictitious, but the scenario is indicative of the situations that may occur.

## Scenario

March 1: Stephanie Lewis, a registered nurse serving in the corporate hospital, is abducted by insurgency forces after serving in her position for a few weeks. Stephanie was removed from an ambulance enroute to an accident victim. The insurgency group claims that they have abducted her for her own safety after learning of a government plot to raid the clinic and kill all the residents and company employees there. The revolutionary group was to be blamed for the encounter. No ransom has been received by rebel radio programs, as of this date.

March 30: The business organization is really becoming concerned. Their representatives are often detained by rebel forces for short periods, but this time there have been no notices, extortion demands, or communiqués from the rebel resistance movement.

April 15: Bob Jonesborough, a Vietnam veteran claiming to be Stephanie Lewis's boyfriend, has been harassing the executives of her employer. He demands to know the plan to *rescue* Stephanie.

May 1: The corporation receives a report that Bob Jonesborough has flown to the country in which his girlfriend is being held. He has been obnoxious to that country's officials and to embassy representatives of the U.S., Chinese, and Russian governments. He is now attempting to recruit a mercenary army in another country on the same continent. This activity is not unlawful in that country, but his activities are probably a violation of the U.S. Neutrality Act.

May 15: The corporation receives a report that Stephanie's home town is raising money for her rescue—sixty thousand dollars has been raised. Rumors abound about the recruitment of a mercenary army.

May 28: A report is received that *Catastrophe* (a tabloid that caters to mercenaries, veterans, and adventure-oriented individuals) is funding a rescue effort. Their action-adventure journalist is on the scene.

June 15: Despairing of never seeing Stephanie again, Stephanie's mother contacts her Congressman. He is in session in Washington, but plans to fly to the country in which Stephanie is held to personally take charge.

June 30: Stephanie's aunt contacts the International Red Cross asking them to petition the revolutionary army. She states that *she* is the official family representative authorized to solicit this aid.

July 15: The corporation contacts an international consulting firm experienced in hostage negotiation to take over and initiate hostage negotiations.

July 27: The insurgency group issues its first communiqué on Stephanie Lewis's situation.

July 28: The public relations office of the terrorist group is contacted in Washington, D.C., to begin opening the necessary contacts overseas. The public relations office is confronted with Stephanie's boyfriend, Stephanie Lewis's home town fundraising chief, *Catastrophe* magazine's representative, a Congressman, Stephanie's mother, Stephanie's aunt, International Red Cross professionals, and the business organization's crisis management consultants.

You can quickly see that the scenario is hectic. Who is in charge? Who has the authority to act? The crisis resolution would have been helped enormously by a simple power-of-attorney authorization, left by the expatriate, authorizing her corporation to act in her behalf. Unauthorized people could then be sent home quickly.

## ■ FAMILY POLICIES

Several different policies can be applied to individuals and families. One family policy requires the immediate transferral of the spouse and children of a hostage victim to a place of safety. As soon as possible, the victim's family should be moved out of the country, usually to their own country.

The establishment of this policy will provide the hostage victim with peace of mind. Related literature is full of examples that promote this type of policy. For example, Geoffrey Jackson, the British Ambassador to Uruguay in the early 1970s, was kidnapped (his driver was killed) and held for 244 days by the Tupamaros. In his book *The Long Night* (also published as *People's Prison* in the U.S.), Ambassador Jackson relates how the Tupamaros taunted him by insisting that they would kidnap his wife if he didn't cooperate. The Tupamaros wanted him to make untrue public statements about the relationship of the United Kingdom to Uruguay, and were using the kidnapping threat as leverage.

Ambassador Jackson and his wife had previously agreed, however, that if either of them were ever kidnapped, the other would leave Uruguay immediately. They had even pre-packed their overnight bags with the necessities. The bags were at home in a closet convenient to the exit. Mrs. Jackson boarded the first British Airways flight out of Montevideo after the kidnapping. It was a great comfort to the Ambassador knowing that she was safe, at home, and surrounded by her family and support network. He got a "double charge" when threatened by the Tupamaros. He knew the Tupamaros could not kidnap his wife because she had left the country.

From interviews and associated literature, it is apparent that the hostages who spent a lot of time worrying about their families were those who had not communicated or planned post-kidnap activities. It is one thing to be concerned about the emotional well-being of your family, but it is quite another to be frightened about their safety.

Established policies are critical tools during a crisis. They get you off to the right start and prevent you from performing inappropriately.

## ■ REFERENCES

1. Kurt Carlson, *One American Must Die* (New York: Congdon and Weed, 1986), 159.
2. Ibid., 161.
3. Brian M. Jenkins, *Terrorism and Personal Protection* (Boston: Butterworth Publishers, 1985), 307.

# PART V

 POST-CRISIS RESPONSE

# 14

## ■■ EMOTIONAL SURVIVAL

Some crises are seemingly never over. The trauma of war, revolution, flood, hurricane, or earthquake is indelibly impressed into the minds of those who have lived and suffered through the experience. There are many psychological trends that can be assessed regarding after-event emotional diagnosis.

Post-traumatic Stress Disorder (PTSD) is probably the diagnosis most often made for an individual who has been subjected to a catastrophic event. Usually, PTSD is a mental trauma versus a physical injury. Among its symptoms is a malady known as *survivor's shock*. The victim feels guilty; they are alive, but others are dead from the same event or simultaneous events. PTSD increases under these circumstances.

If you had been shot, burned, or suffered a broken bone during the course of a crisis, a treatment program would be immediately offered. However, stress, burnout, PTSD, combat fatigue, and other manifestations of a damaged or altered psyche are much more difficult to heal and diagnosis is often difficult.

Many mental health professionals have little or no experience in this area. Diagnosis is especially difficult when there was no single catastrophic event. Living in a life-threatening environment for a long time can be even more damaging than experiencing a single catastrophic event. This observation was immediately made by health care professionals for returning Vietnam veterans. PTSD has also been referenced in the literature in reference to violent crime and rape victims who continue to live in the environment in which they were attacked.

Congress has ensured that natural disaster victims are treated for PTSD, free of charge, within the continental U.S. or its territories. Military personnel are likewise treated for service-related trauma in military hospitals.

Why should corporations do less for their trauma victims? In many circles, the mere mention of mental health professionals is an anathema. There is a tremendous stigma attached to psychological or psychiatric treatment. Many people think, "The very idea! A real man shouldn't have to see a shrink and only a weak woman should see one." Unfortunately, this attitude is pervasive enough that PTSD treatment is often avoided when it is obviously necessary.

Businesspeople seeking emotional help should not be labeled as insecure or weak. As long as inappropriate myths and misconceptions prevail about counseling, the individuals who need it the most will avoid it like a plague. This attitude also causes revictimization. This labeling adds additional stresses to their trauma.

Add the intensity of the crisis, peer responses, and all the guilt if something went wrong, and you have another crisis on your hands. Sometimes a complete mental breakdown occurs under these circumstances. Let us not neglect our surviving victims, their families, and those closely related to a tragic incident.

In a crisis and during a hostage negotiation there is a *tremendous* burden on those involved. "Is my judgment sound? Is my understanding correct? Am I discerning this event as I should? Am I on target today? What could I do wrong to cause the hostage to die?"

The events that stimulate PTSD include natural disasters, criminal attacks, and political crises. Natural events include flood, earthquake, fire, automobile accidents, and personal tragedies. Criminal attacks include the violent crimes, such as robbery, rape, murder, and kidnapping. However, an individual who has been burglarized on several occasions or who has had her car stolen four or five times may also become a cumulative stress victim. Political crises include war, revolution, proselytizing, incarceration, kidnapping by insurgents, or a massive evacuation.

## ■ RICHARD FARLEY'S ANALOGY

Dr. Richard Farley, a clinical psychologist, used this analogy to discuss PTSD.

> A deep-sea diver, if placed in a rapid descent, must be concerned with equalizing pressure in his eardrum to keep it and the sinuses from rupturing. Once at depth, if the diver is then suddenly brought to the surface, the rapid decompression can cause the *bends.* No one blames the diver for contracting the bends; this very painful and potentially fatal circumstance is the result of nitrogen bubbles forming in the blood stream due to rapid decompression.
>
> Trauma can be interpreted as a rapid psychological compression and decompression. PTSD is the injury that can occur during psychological decompression.[1]

PTSD injures the psyche; it injures our appraisal system. PTSD also lowers our ability to take or accept additional stress.

There is a rough parity in our ability to handle a threat and the reality of experiencing the threat. The stress level may be minimized. After the trauma, threat apperception increases significantly, but the coping resources are impaired. Your perception of reality is remarkably affected after a major incident. You may discover that the same stresses you have handled for years are now simply too much for you.

# ■ HOW TO RECOGNIZE PTSD

There are four categories that help mental health professionals or even laypersons recognize the onset of PTSD—emotional, cognitive, physiological, and behavioral.

## Emotional

A person may be numb from her experience. She may have been kidnapped or seen someone killed. Perhaps the victim was in a natural disaster in which many people perished. The PTSD victim may be reliving the trauma in her daydreams and nightmares. PTSD victims actually feel that the trauma is reoccurring, even after they are in a safe environment. They are anxious, afraid, and have phobias (totally unrealistic fears).

Phobic personalities may have severe mood swings and act in a manner similar to the manic depressive. They are ready to fight the world one minute and in the next minute they are scared to face the world at all. They may be friendly and open in the morning and very irritable and moody during the afternoon. They may be ashamed that they lived through an incident when someone much more "worthy" perished during the encounter. They feel guilty that they survived, yet they are glad they did. Still, they may be incredibly sad and depressed over those who did not survive.

## Cognitive

Cognition is the act of recognizing that something is wrong. Cognition includes memory, perception, and judgement. One example of cognitive difficulty is indicated by the post-trauma personality who daydreams incessantly. Another cognitive difficulty is evidenced by the inability of the victim to concentrate. A person who once had an excellent memory for detail may no longer remember simple things, such as important appointments or signing outgoing mail before sealing the envelope. A person who once prided herself on good diction may now make major mistakes in grammar and syntax.

It may be difficult to carry on a normal conversation with the trauma victim. Their cognitive difficulties prevent them from recalling what was just said or the topic currently under discussion. They may keep refocusing on particular issues that have been already carefully discussed.

Perhaps you set a date for your quarterly business meeting at a particular location. This was not a tentative decision. The decision has been made. Maybe the event has even been widely publicized in organizational newsletters. But your PTSD victim keeps asking "when are we holding our business meeting? Did you say where it will be held?" This person is just a little out of step with reality.

The victim may be easily confused, think of particulars repetitively, and may have a great deal of difficulty in making simple, relatively unimportant decisions. Deciding what to eat for supper may be a major decision for the traumatized person.

### Physiological

The physiological difficulties associated with PTSD can also be quite acute. Problems can arise that never existed before. The primary changes occur in eating and sleeping. The trauma victim may be impaired in his sexual relations as well. A kidnap victim may have trained himself, during captivity, to not think of sexual things. If the captivity was prolonged, a male may encounter impotence when faced with a sexual situation upon returning home. The female may simply need tenderness and a reaffirmation of love, rather than physical expressions of intimacy.

A loss of appetite is a normal aftereffect of trauma. Diet habits may also run in the other direction. A person who stayed slim all of her life may now want to snack all of the time and may begin to gain weight. Gastrointestinal disorders and frequency of urination are also another response to trauma. The nervous system continues to influence normal internal processes long after the traumatic event is over.

Insomnia may also be experienced. The former victim lost the sleep habits of a lifetime. He could also sleep excessively. If there is stress, the recovering victim may go to sleep in a chair or on the sofa, rather than waiting for bed.

Many PTSD patients no longer have any energy and may catch colds, flu, and viruses easily. A mile jog may place them in a state of exhaustion, whereas they could run for 10 miles before the trauma occurred. Before the trauma, an exercise regime energized them; today, it saps all of their energy and depletes their reserves.

Some victims may have anxiety attacks as well. They may suffer chest and arm pain—the symptoms of a heart attack. Often, the heart will beat rapidly, they may hyperventilate, or they may experience severe headaches or migraines, whereas they never suffered these symptoms prior to the traumatic event. These physical problems may persist for an extended period of time.

### Behavioral

Many former victims dramatically alter their daily behavioral patterns. Some may become workaholics and overactive to ensure that uncomfortable thoughts or feelings are repressed. Their daily schedule does not allow them the opportunity for contemplation or reflection; they do not want to think about this period in their lives.

Some victims demand an immediate job assignment, but most corporations want them to rest for a few weeks. These victims cause problems for the corporation because they *insist* that they are all right.

Many former victims withdraw from social situations. They may have been personable or even extroverted all of their lives. Now they just want to be left alone. They are afraid that someone will want them to talk about their experiences and they do not want to talk about it. Some victims want to discuss their experiences all the time. This is the time when they need the most help, however.

Some former victims alter other behavioral patterns. Upon returning home, some POWs and corporate terrorist victims discover that they have accumulated a large amount of savings. Their salaries were being banked for them. Some corporations give large bonuses to victims as this prevents potential lawsuits and serves as a reward for extraordinary service under adverse conditions. Now, upon having so much money for the first time, they may become flamboyant spenders and purchase luxury or sports cars, top-level executive clothing, and exotic accessories and furnishings. They may cease value-shopping, as they once did.

A former victim may also find himself accident-prone. Fender-benders, falling, burns and cuts in the kitchen, stubbing toes, and a variety of other fairly painful behavioral manifestations may occur.

Some victims may also neglect good health and grooming habits. They may brush their teeth less or even forget to brush at all. They may bathe less often, even to the point where body odor makes associates feel uncomfortable. Men may stop shaving their faces and women may neglect shaving their legs and underarm areas. Fingernails may be dirty and untrimmed. These basic hygiene habits are just not important to the trauma victim any more.

They may be sloppy dressers as well. They may put together ensembles that are not color-coordinated. These symptoms are indicators of posttrauma stress, particularly if prior to the crisis the individual was always well-groomed, clean, and manicured. These observations are indications that the person may need help, compassion, and assistance. If this person is to be "rescued," he needs the help of a qualified mental health professional.

The last symptom of PTSD mentioned here has to do with the proper handling of organizational paperwork, policies, and rules or regulations. Former victims sometimes come home with a total indifference or intolerance for the mundane rules and regulations that most organizations require. With this attitude, however, they may now fail to file their visa extensions, their annual tax returns, and the business organization's required monthly reports. These actions are now trivial to them. The organization should not ignore indications, because by ignoring the problem, the victim's actions are reinforced.

# ■ PSYCHOLOGICAL DECOMPRESSION

Dr. Farley made another observation in reference to the problems of Vietnam trauma victims, who perhaps had more difficulty adjusting to civilian life than the trauma victims of other hostile actions. Briefly, Dr. Farley states that in World War I, World War II, and the Korean War, military personnel traveled home on crew ships. These ships were large, heavy, and slow. These people normally sailed for 30 to 40 days from their foreign port until they docked stateside. Some, stationed in Africa or in the Far East, sailed for even longer periods of time.

Many of these men and women had experienced common battlefield and sea combat trials. They could discuss them, relive them, or laugh about them during the long cruise home. The trip, itself, was therapeutic. It offered a period of decompression.

In Vietnam, however, military personnel were put on air cargo planes and jets. From the jungles to home in 30 hours or less, they were left without the opportunity to decompress.[2]

*All* victims need to decompress, even if they have not lived in a dangerous zone. It is stressful to leave a foreign locale, return to the states, suffer jet lag, and begin to visit your office within a week or two of your return.

Organizations need to review their policies toward trauma victims. With the possible exception of continuing the education of children, businesspeople should go on a stateside vacation on their return, prior to getting involved in any administrative responsibility.

As previously mentioned, stress does not have to come from a single catastrophic event. Cumulative stress is also a problem. In one recent 8-day period, Lima, Peru, reported more than 100 bombings. The safety level and security perceptions of Americans are very high there; they should be. Expatriates are also stressed about the safety of their children and the security of their mates. These cumulative stresses can be just as damaging as the stress suffered from a catastrophe.

# ■ CORPORATE RESPONSE TO TRAUMA

Remember that the symptoms of PTSD are not the victim's fault. Difficulty in coping, helplessness in accomplishing routine tasks, and the accompanying feelings of depression need to be resolved. The organization must see to it that this is accomplished. Appendix 4 addresses the policy.

The support necessary for the victim is predicated upon the analysis of several variables. These variables include

- the severity and duration of the trauma,
- the degree of helplessness or control experienced by the victim,
- the impact of assigned responsibility for other personnel,
- the stability of the survivor's support structure in their family and friends, and
- pre-trauma personality variables.

Every stress victim and every potential stress victim should be interviewed by a qualified mental health professional as soon as possible after their return. They should be given another check-up in about 6 months— sooner if it appears appropriate. In some cases, repressed stress will surface years later. If qualified counselors can help at this time, the period of healing can be lessened considerably.

The organization should also assign an advocate to the former victim. This person should have known the victim prior to the trauma and should have a mature and caring disposition. The purpose of this assignment is to help the victim. The advocate can approach the organization in the victim's behalf if there is a need, instead of the victim doing it personally.

If the invisible wound of PTSD is carefully treated, its damage to the individual and the organization can be minimized.

## ■ DR. FARLEY'S TIPS TO ADVOCATES

1. Be supportive and nonjudgmental. The survivor is usually his own harshest judge.
2. Maintain strict confidentiality. Do not violate the survivor's trust. Shared topics must stay within the strictest confidence.
3. Be open to what may be a full and oftentimes contradictory range of emotional expression. Even if the feelings are unfair or uncalled for, remember that to be supportive means to be receptive to the complete range of the survivor's expressions. Survivors need friends to assure them that the world is back in its proper place. Speak the truth in a sensitive way and not as a dictator. Tolerate their feelings and behaviors within the confines of good judgment.
4. Remind the survivor that it is normal to experience conflicting emotions simultaneously. The horror of recounting specific events, joy over surviving, grief for those who may not have been so

fortunate, the guilt over not having performed to one's expectations are all normal.

5. Current research indicates that the proximity to a crisis can precipitate symptoms of PTSD in children. If working with children, realize that they have the same need to express their feelings and make the world make sense again, as do their adult counterparts. Play with them; encourage creative story telling. Children need trust to help them sort out what has happened. Do not shield them by pretending nothing happened. It will not help them in the long run.

6. Be the survivor's liaison to friends, family, and your organization.

7. Assist the survivor in planning for the immediate future. Deal with issues such as needed time off from work and other responsibilities, and coordinate medical care. Be careful of the survivor's premature desire to "get back in the saddle."

8. If closely involved with the survivor, take care of yourself, too. Burnout can be a very real problem. Be sure your own support system is intact. Be ready to admit it if you find yourself in over your head with the survivor's issues. Requesting help from a professional counselor may be a necessity.[3]

# ■ REFERENCES

1. Dr. Richard Farley, "Contingency Preparation Consultants Seminar" (Dallas, Texas, 1988).
2. Ibid.
3. Ibid.

# APPENDICES

 SAMPLE POLICIES

# APPENDIX 1

## ■■ CRISIS MANAGEMENT

### ■ INTENTION

The corporate governing board wants to create a coordinated and unified leadership response to any major crisis affecting the Board of Directors, its facilities, its staff, or their families. The leadership will be free to respond to the needs of the crisis with a clear understanding of its responsibility and its authority. The response may be flexible, depending upon the location of the crisis, the type of crisis, and the management resources available to resolve the crisis.

A CMT will be created to allow the majority of the organization's staff and resources to remain committed to the primary tasks and objectives of the organization, rather than being continually diverted throughout the crisis response.

### ■ POLICY

It is the policy of this Board of Directors that in the event that any of its members, their families, staff, or facilities are threatened by a significant crisis that a CMT will be appointed by the Corporate Chief Executive Officer. The CMT will handle the crisis from its inception and through all negotiation, resolution, and follow-up activities.

The establishment of the CMT may be authorized by the Board of Directors when the Corporation is faced with a crisis that is likely to be extended in time and that will probably demand an abnormal commitment of resources, or when the actual or potential consequences of the crisis seriously threaten lives or the continuance of business operations in a particular area.

This policy of the Board of Directors also mandates that upon establishment of a CMT, all other members of the Corporation *shall* refer all information, suggestions, and intelligence materials relating to the crisis to the CMT. All members and employees of the Corporation or its sub-units are to refrain from making public comments in reference to the crisis. All members and employees of the Corporation are to refrain from taking any action relating to the crisis without the specific prior approval and direction of the CMT.

The CMT will include a Chairperson who will answer to the Chief Executive Officer or designee. The CMT will also include a press officer and members familiar with the culture and language of the crisis location. All appointees will prioritize the crisis event, setting aside all other normal duties where appropriate, even to the point of devoting full-time attention to the crisis. The CMT should be small enough to function well and be delegated sufficient authority to cut through the organizational bureaucracy. All skills necessary will be recruited from within the organization whenever possible.

The Chief Executive Officer is authorized to select consultants from outside the corporate structure to aid the CMT or to function as hostage negotiator when unusual crisis conditions exist or when the Corporation is confronted with hostage-takers, terrorists, guerrillas, or other criminals.

A CMT fund of $30,000 is placed in escrow as of the date of the approval of the policy by the Board of Directors. This fund will be advanced, as needed, for the appropriate use by the CMT.

# APPENDIX 2

## ■■ COMMUNICATION DURING A CRISIS

### ■ INTENTION

The flow of information during a crisis must be directed and controlled. The experiences of other corporations, organizations, governments, and business entities indicates that the control of rumors is of primary importance. Secondary crises may well be created whenever information is not controlled by the CMT. All incoming information must be directed to the CMT. All outgoing information must be monitored and *controlled* to prevent the release of confidential information and to control the spread of rumors.

### ■ POLICY

It is the policy of this Board of Directors that all information, intelligence, data, and suggestions relating to a crisis *shall* be directed to the CMT at the earliest possible moment. Any staff member receiving information shall forward the information to the team. Any staff member with a suggestion shall forward the proposal, information, or suggestion to the CMT immediately. The CMT member responsible for receiving this information shall be promptly identified through organizational memoranda. Any special phone numbers of the CMT shall be posted promptly.

It is further the policy of this Board of Directors that all information released to the news media will be accomplished by the CMT. No member of the Corporation outside of the CMT is authorized to make any statement that relates in any way to an ongoing crisis. All media inquiries shall be referred to the CMT. Only the official designee of the CMT shall make releases in its behalf. All releases will be carefully *written* and released to the press.

# APPENDIX 3

## ■■ FAMILIES OF HOSTAGES

### ■ INTENTION

The Board of Directors shall attempt to balance the interests of the hostage, the needs of his family, and the ongoing operations of the business. The primary objective throughout the event will be the safe release of the hostage and the safety of the family.

The experience of previous hostages, their families, hostage negotiators, and crisis managers shall be examined. It has been discovered that the hostages who know that their families have been evacuated to a safe country or location have better adjusted to their captivity. They were assured that their families were safe even as they lived in bondage and were taunted by threats from their captors.

The Board of Directors also recognizes that the presence of the family near the scene of negotiations can be disruptive and may even delay the resolution of the crisis. The Board of Directors also recognizes that the very special physical, emotional, and psychological needs of the hostage's family must be met.

### ■ POLICY

It is the policy of this Board of Directors that in the event of a hostage seizure of its personnel, the family of the hostage will be evacuated to a safe location as soon as possible. In most cases, the safe location will be the family's home country. This policy will be waived only if a determination is made that an evacuation of the family is not in the best interests of the hostage or his family.

It is the policy of this Board of Directors that a staff member shall be assigned to work with the family throughout the period of the crisis. This staff member shall provide news and information to the family and take whatever steps are possible to minimize the stress and consequences of the crisis on the family.

Professional counseling is authorized for the victim's family even during the crisis' inception. (See Appendix 4 for a sample policy on psychological consultation.)

# APPENDIX 4

## ■■ PSYCHOLOGICAL CONSULTATION

### ■ INTENTION

The Board of Directors recognizes that personnel who undergo traumatic events or live in dangerous circumstances for an extended period of time may suffer emotional reactions. These reactions may become quite destructive if untreated. It is the Board's intention that *all* of those directly involved in traumatic events shall receive competent evaluation from a crisis-accredited psychologist or mental health professional. Should any post-crisis treatment be appropriate, the Board of Directors will help provide it.

Personnel shall not be intrusively selected. All participants in a crisis matter may be evaluated, including but not limited to the victim, the extended family of the victim, and organizational personnel directly impacted by the crisis, such as CMT members and the hostage negotiator.

Any psychological evaluation, intervention, or treatment shall be conducted in a confidential and professional matter. The sole objective of this action is the treatment of existing trauma and the prevention of future or debilitating trauma associated with the crisis.

### ■ POLICY

It is the policy of this Board of Directors that those who are directly involved in a crisis shall receive an initial and follow-up evaluation from a qualified mental health professional. These evaluations shall occur immediately following a crisis and again 6 to 12 months following the crisis, unless specified otherwise by a competent mental health professional.

The evaluations and any treatment will be confidential between the individual and the mental health professional. The Board of Directors will fund the examinations, evaluations, treatment program, and any travel or living expenses relative to this program.

Although the individuals who receive evaluation may vary from incident to incident, in each case, the victim, the immediate family, the CMT Chairperson, and the hostage negotiator shall receive this evaluation.

# APPENDIX 5

## ■■ POST-CRISIS EVALUATION

### ■ INTENTION

Every opportunity should be taken to improve the Board of Director's response to any crisis situation. Each crisis, and the Board of Director's response to it, shall be reviewed and critiqued to identify those qualities that were strong and appropriate, so that they can be further developed and repeated in the future. The Board of Directors also wants to focus on those areas of weakness, so that these can be eliminated or remedied through reallocation of resources, appropriate training, or policy changes.

This policy will also aid the Corporation when individual staff members resign or retire and will not be available for future corporate involvement. It is not the intention of the Board of Directors that individuals be blamed or criticized, we simply wish to learn from our mistakes.

The overall intention of the policy is for the Board of Directors to be better prepared each time there is a crisis, so that the crisis can be resolved as efficiently as possible.

### ■ POLICY

Within 60 days of the resolution of a crisis, a formal evaluation shall be conducted. This evaluation shall be made by an individual appointed by the Executive Director of the Board of Directors and should not be conducted by any person reporting directly to any individual whose actions in the crisis will be reviewed.

The evaluation shall address causal factors in the crisis, initial responses to the crisis, and the performance of the CMT. The evaluation should address those areas of strength in order that these may be repeated in any future crisis and those areas of weakness so that they may be improved upon or eliminated. The evaluation shall also identify any areas in which policies should be established or changed.

# APPENDIX 6

## ■■ EVACUATION

### ■ INTENTION

The Board of Directors recognizes that the conditions in certain countries may, on occasion, become unacceptable for continuing operation. These events occur during wartime and during periods of intensive guerrilla or terrorist operation. Because of problems relating to telephone and radio communications during periods of violence, the Board of Directors delegates the authority to evacuate a particular area to the individual staff member.

### ■ POLICY

The decision to evacuate a particular area shall be made by the appropriate administrator. If the emergency is sudden and normal communications to the administrator are not possible, the individual staff member is authorized to make the decision to evacuate if he feels that it would be unsafe to remain at his current location.

# APPENDIX 7

## ■■ CRISIS MANAGEMENT TRAINING

### ■ INTENTION

It is the intention of this policy to provide appropriate leaders with training to prepare them to respond to crisis situations.

### ■ POLICY

All management personnel responsible for the continents of Africa, Asia, Latin and South America, and other locations where frequent violence occurs shall be required to attend training courses on incident avoidance and victim survival. Individual organizational managers in countries or locations of continuing violence shall also be required to attend this training session within the next 12 months.

The Corporation shall make available library resources (including video and audio tapes) concerning terrorism, crime prevention, and guerrilla activities.

# APPENDIX 8

## ■■ HOSTAGE NEGOTIATION

### ■ INTENTION

The U.S. Government and the representatives of some other western nations have, on occasion, recommended that an effective terrorism policy is to never capitulate to terrorism. Their interpretation is not to negotiate with terrorists and to never pay any extortion demand. On the other hand, we now know that some of these same governments have negotiated with terrorist groups for a great number of years.

The Board of Directors also recognizes that negotiating, in some cultures, is a way of life and a calculated way of doing business or resolving problems. We further understand that negotiation is the most common means of effecting the release of a victim.[1]

### ■ POLICY

The Board of Directors is authorized to conduct negotiations as it deems necessary to save the life of any staff member abducted while on official business of this Corporation. It will employ such consultants and negotiators as it deems appropriate.

---

[1]Richard W. Kobetz and H.H.A. Cooper, *Target Terrorism: Providing Protective Services* (Gaithersburg, Maryland: The International Association of Chiefs of Police, 1978), 69.

# APPENDIX 9

## ■■ EMERGENCY POWER-OF-ATTORNEY AUTHORIZATION

### ■ INTENTION

The Board of Directors recognizes that there are inordinate and extraordinary circumstances occurring during times of warfare, violence, criminal activity, guerrilla activity, and terrorist activity. Further, it is recognized that individuals, families, and managers may not have the necessary expertise to deal with these issues.

It is recognized that, on occasion, certain families and individuals have intruded into sensitive negotiations involving the life and the safety of hostage members of our Corporation. In some cases, family members have acted in ways detrimental to the best continued interests of the hostages and of our Corporation. To ensure the Corporation's continued success, the Board of Directors, after much discussion and consultation, invokes the following policy:

### ■ POLICY

Prior to accepting a foreign assignment, the Board of Directors *requires* that its employees sign a power-of-attorney agreement giving this Board of Directors the exclusive authority to deal directly or indirectly with whatever entities that may hold the employee captive.

This Board of Directors will make every reasonable effort to keep family members informed of all progress. Should an individual family member become intrusive, the power-of-attorney agreement will be invoked to authorize legal restraint against that individual.

This Board of Directors shall have two priorities in all negotiations. The first priority is the life of the hostage. The second priority is the continuing business interests of this Corporation in that country. In keeping with this policy, the Board of Directors has the authority to appoint outside professional consultants to assist in reconciling the situation.

# APPENDIX 10

## ■■ RANSOM PAYMENTS AND EXTORTION DEMANDS

### ■ INTENTION

This Board of Directors recognizes the deterrent effect of a policy prohibiting the payment of ransom or yielding to an extortion demand. This Board of Directors also recognizes the need for a flexible response to negotiation activities. Rather than dictate absolutes, this Board of Directors maintains its prerogative to retain the authority to make a decision concerning ransom or extortion demands that is in the best interests of the affected personnel and the Corporation.

This Board of Directors recognizes that our Negotiation Policy may well enable us to serve mankind in a unique and special way. Negotiations for large sums of money which may be used to arm or train violent groups are obviously unacceptable. In some cases, the negotiated settlement of an ongoing crisis may be something that can serve mankind. Blankets to the poor people of an impoverished region, food for the hungry, and health care for the needy may all be negotiated in lieu of assets that may be used in ongoing violence.

We also recognize that, sometimes, revolutionary groups misunderstand the availability of liquid assets available to the Corporation. They expect great resources to become available to them, such as they have received from many businesses and individuals in the past. When the revolutionary group holding the hostage realizes that these resources are not quickly available, as in the case of a small or developing business, the group is often at an impasse to admit that mistake. Sometimes a mere "token" payment of the expenses of "protecting" the employee is all that is required to conclude the event satisfactorily. By saying "No" and "Never" to terrorists, we will be limiting our options considerably. If at all possible, alternative resolutions *not* involving the payment of ransoms or extortion demands will be sought. The final decision on the payment of ransom or extortion, or any concession to other demands issued through hostage-taking, shall be made by the CMT, with the approval of the Board of Directors' Chief Executive Officer and all Board members. Our *stated* policy shall continue to comply with the U.S. Policy. But we are flexible; we do not state we will never pay ransoms.

# ■ POLICY

We are fundamentally opposed to the concept of paying ransom or extortion demands. We hold to the belief that this Corporation should not yield to extortion demands issued through the use of hostage-taking misadventures or the ongoing threat of violence.

# ■■ INDEX